SOLVING THE ESG PARADOX

THE NEW MEASUREMENT PARADIGM

notionpress.com

INDIA • SINGAPORE • MALAYSIA

SOLVING THE ESG PARADOX

THE NEW MEASUREMENT PARADIGM

ESG QUANTA CALIBRATOR

Dr. Alex Philip

notionpress.com

INDIA • SINGAPORE • MALAYSIA

ISBN
Paperback 979-8-90451-366-5
Hardcase 979-8-90451-670-3

TABLE OF CONTENTS

This Book is dedicated to my Parents,

Late Mr.Philip George

&

Mrs. Sophy Philip.

ACKNOWLEDGMENTS

I am deeply grateful to all those who have supported me throughout my journey as an author. My heartfelt thanks first go to Almighty God, whose strength and perseverance enabled me to complete my doctoral degree.

I wish to extend my sincere appreciation to Mr. Jimmy K Thomas for his invaluable guidance, thoughtful advice, and constructive feedback throughout the publication process. I am equally indebted to my research mentor, Prof. Dr. Saša Petar, Ph.D., whose expertise, encouragement, and critical insights were essential to the success of my research endeavors.

My gratitude also goes to Mr. Markus Blanka-Graff, Chief Financial Officer of Kuehne + Nagel International AG; Ms. Christine Wiederkehr-Luther, Global Head of Sustainability at Kuehne + Nagel International AG; and Mr. Narasimhan Damodaran, National Project Logistics Customer Excellence Manager at Kuehne Nagel (P) Ltd. India. Their invaluable insights, guidance, and unwavering support played a significant role during my research journey.

Finally, I am deeply appreciative of the encouragement and assistance provided by everyone who contributed to this accomplishment.

Thank you all, and may you be blessed for your support.

FOREWORD

When Alex and I first met at our head offices in Switzerland to discuss his project, it quickly became clear how important this work would be. We talked about the opportunities global companies have to do the right things in the dimension of ESG—while also being recognized for doing so.

The Sustainable Development Goals (SDGs) are unequivocally of substantial benefit to society and must constitute an integral component of our collective global agenda.

Operating a global network of affiliates requires navigating a multitude of regulations in every country of operation. ESG rating agencies have become a key reference point for investors and shareholders, yet their assessments vary significantly—not only across countries but also across agencies. While we cannot influence the methodologies applied by rating agencies, we also cannot fully meet global requirements through isolated, country-level solutions.

Unlike financial rating agencies, which apply uniform market rules to ensure comparability and methodological consistency, the ESG landscape lacks such transparency and standardization.

As legislators began to introduce ESG-related norms, it became evident that the reporting and rating ecosystem was extremely diverse in regulatory density, reporting requirements, and methodological maturity. To achieve meaningful ratings—ones that reliably measure progress and provide comparable benchmarks within and across industries—we must contextualize information and calibrate assessments accordingly.

Effective stakeholder management requires consistent and relevant information. Calibrated ESG scores offer precisely that: data that informs better decisions and enables better outcomes. While the ESG agenda has been embedded in the strategies of most global companies, the responsibility to develop and advance ESG practices has largely been left to the companies themselves. In this gap between regulatory ambitions, corporate initiatives, and available information, rating agencies have stepped in—resulting in a wide spectrum of rating outcomes for the very same company, especially for global enterprises.

Within business management, the forecasting of economic and operational key performance indicators (KPIs) is fundamental. Organizations rely on KPIs, continuous improvement mechanisms, structured risk management, and operational transparency to steer performance. Accurate measurement and iterative feedback processes are therefore essential.

In contrast, it quickly became evident that ESG metrics are characterized by significant uncertainty—stemming from data gaps, inconsistent rating methodologies, and heterogeneous regulatory requirements.

Put simply, assuming the "accuracy" of ESG metrics is logically untenable. They cannot be presumed to be perfectly calibrated; instead, they require quantifiable probabilistic confidence levels rather than unexamined assumptions.

Alex being in financial controlling for decades, deeply rooted in the world of financial KPIs with detailed expertise in finance for multinational companies, shared this concern and started working on his idea for the ‚ESG Quanta Calibrator'.

Our objective was to establish a methodology for ESG assessment that mirrors the robustness applied to financial performance, reporting, and forecasting. For leadership teams of global enterprises, the transparency and reliability of information are crucial. We cannot allow management decisions to be influenced by methodological biases embedded within ESG rating agencies' assessments.

It was within this context that Alex advanced the concept of a normalized calibration framework across ESG rating methodologies—acknowledging the prevalence of uncalibrated variability. This recognition formed the foundation of his subsequent work.

A normative calibration framework would allow rating agencies to maintain their methodologies while also acknowledging the diverse regulatory landscapes companies operate in. This is an obvious—but highly challenging—solution.

If you want to gain relevant reference points for your own company's ESG development, status, and progress—by comparing different rating methodologies, consolidating billions of data points, and applying a normalized calibration to produce sustainable, verifiable, and auditable ESG information—then this book is essential reading.

Markus Blanka-Graff
Chief Financial Officer
Kuehne + Nagel Group
Switzerland

WHY ESG RATINGS NEED RECALIBRATION NOW?

Solving the Calibration Paradox

Presenting the New Global ESG Rating Formula

ESG Quanta Calibrator

INTRODUCTION

THE CALIBRATION PARADOX IN ESG

The concept of ESG (Environment, Social and Governance) is not a novel one, its roots tracing back many decades. However, it was in 2004, following the publication of the United Nation's seminal report titled "Who Cares Wins," that ESG assumed its contemporary form. In the two decades since, governments across the globe have come to appreciate not only the necessity but also the profound significance of this ideology, enacting diverse legislation to support its widespread adoption. This initiative has seen rampant growth in recent years, evidenced by the fact that most of the Fortune 500 companies now publish ESG reports in tandem with their annual financial statements.

According to "Who Cares Wins," sound corporate governance and robust risk management frameworks are fundamental prerequisites for the successful implementation of strategies and policies that address environmental and social challenges.

The logistics sector occupies a pivotal position in a nation's economic development, yet it also poses significant implications for environmental quality, being acknowledged as a major consumer of energy. On a global scale, logistics are integral to efficient supply chain management and serve as a substantial driver of economic growth (Lean et al., 2014). However, logistics activities can also adversely affect environmental standards, a reality that has prompted considerable debate and analysis in recent years.

The concept of ESG performance is designed to offer a comprehensive assessment of how effectively a company is managing the risks and opportunities associated with environmental, social, and governance concerns (Christensen et al., 2022). Notably, a study by Statista (2023) revealed that in 2021, the transportation industry ranked second in terms of carbon dioxide emissions, accounting for 20.2% of the total. The power generation sector led with 37.7%, followed by - other industrial activities at 21.4%, building at 9%, and all other sectors collectively at 11.7%.

Diving further, the study disaggregated transportation-related carbon dioxide emissions as follows: passenger cars accounted for 39%, medium and heavy trucks for 23%, shipping accounted for 11%, aviation 9%, buses and minibuses 7%, light commercial vehicles for 5%, two/three wheelers for 3%, and rail for 3%.

ENVIRONMENT

Global warming constitutes a subject demanding immediate and decisive action to secure the survival of the planet. Defined as the protracted increase in the Earth's average temperature, global warming is principally driven by the emission of greenhouse gases (GHG) into the atmosphere.

According to the Center for Climate and Energy Solutions, the global anthropogenic greenhouse gas emissions ratio in 2015 was as follows: carbon dioxide (CO_2) 76%, methane (CH_4) 16%, nitrous oxide (N_2O) 6%, and hydrofluorocarbon (HFC), Sulphur hexafluoride (SF_6), and related gases collectively at 2%. The potency of atmospheric gases in contributing to global warming is determined by two main characteristics: their ability to absorb and re-emit energy (their "radiative efficiency") and their atmospheric lifetime, which is the duration they persist before being removed by natural processes such as chemical reactions.

These attributes are incorporated within the metric of Global Warming Potential (GWP), which measures the radiative impact i.e., the warming effect of each unit of gas, by weight, over a specified period, commonly one hundred years and expresses this effect relative to that of carbon dioxide (CO_2). Gases with high GWP will induce more warming than an equivalent mass of CO_2 over the same period. A gas that persists in the atmosphere for a long time, even with moderate radiative efficiency, may exert more warming than a gas that, although highly efficient radiatively, is removed quickly from the atmosphere. This distinction is reflected in GWP values.

Despite carbon dioxide's comparatively modest GWP among the principal greenhouse gases, the marked increase in its atmospheric concentration due to human activity has rendered it the chief driver of global warming. Similarly, methane has contributed significantly to recent warming trends, not because of its GWP alone but owing to substantial increases in emissions.

Table 1: Global Warming Potential and Atmospheric Lifetime of Major Greenhouse Gases

Global Warming Potential and Atmospheric Lifetime of Major Greenhouse Gases			
SOURCE: Fifth Assessment Report (Intergovernmental Panel on Climate Change, 2014).			
Greenhouse gas	Chemical formula	Global Warming Potential, 100-year time horizon	Atmospheric Lifetime (years)
Carbon Dioxide	CO_2	1	100*
Methane	CH_4	25	12
Nitrous Oxide	N_2O	265	121
Chlorofluorocarbon-12 (CFC-12)	CCl_2F_2	10,200	100
Hydrofluorocarbon-23 (HFC-23)	CHF_3	12,400	222
Sulfur Hexafluoride	SF_6	23,500	3,200
Nitrogen Trifluoride	NF_3	16,100	500

According to the Intergovernmental Panel on Climate Change (IPCC), there is more than 50% probability that global temperature rise will reach or exceed 1.5 degrees Celsius (2.7 degrees Fahrenheit) between 2021 and 2040 across the scenarios studied. Under a high emissions pathway, this threshold may be attained even sooner; between 2018 and 2037.

Net Zero refers to the equilibrium where the quantity of greenhouse gases removed from the atmosphere equals the quantity emitted by human activity. In contrast, carbon neutrality pertains specifically to removing an amount of CO_2 equivalent to that emitted, typically through absorption by carbon sinks. Carbon sinks, such as oceans and forests are systems that absorb and store more carbon from the atmosphere than they emit.

The ocean absorbs CO_2 through photosynthesis by phytoplankton (plant-like organisms). Additionally, carbon dioxide dissolves in seawater, forming carbonic acid, which subsequently breaks apart to produce bicarbonate ions and hydrogen ions. Sea algae, owing to their rapid growth and extensive coverage, absorb more CO_2 than terrestrial trees. The Southern Ocean, encircling Antarctica, serves as a particularly significant carbon sink, absorbing more atmospheric carbon than it releases, largely because cold water is more effective at dissolving CO_2 than warm water.

The Paris Agreement on Climate Change and the United Nations Sustainable Development Goals are two key topics that should be addressed when discussing environmental issues.

PARIS AGREEMENT ON CLIMATE CHANGE:

In 2015, parties to the United Nations Framework Convention on Climate Change (UNFCCC) reached an agreement at Paris, for combating climate change and to accelerate and intensify the actions and investments needed for a sustainable low carbon future. This conference, which is the main decision- making body of UNFCCC is known as Conference of Parties (COP). The Paris agreement is a legally binding international treaty in climate change, which is adopted by 196 parties during COP 21.

The main aim of Paris agreement is to strengthen the global response to the threat of climate change by keeping a global temperature rise in this century well below 2 degree Celsius above pre-industrial level and to pursue efforts to limit the temperature increase even further to 1.5 degree Celsius. Additionally, the agreement aims to increase the ability of countries to deal with the impacts of climate change, and at making finance flow consistent with a low GHG emissions and climate resilient pathway. To achieve this temperature goal, parties aim to reach global peaking of GHG as soon as possible.

Pre Industrial period is the time before starting the industrial revolution, which is generally considered from the year AD 1750 to AD 1850.

SOME OF THE OTHER KEY ASPECTS OF PARIS AGREEMENTS ARE AS BELOW:

- Global peaking and climate neutrality: To achieve this temperature goal, parties aim to reach global peaking of greenhouse gas emissions as soon as possible, recognising peaking will take longer for developing country parties, so as to achieve a balance between anthropogenic emissions by sources and removals by sinks of GHG in the second half of the century.
- Mitigation: The Paris agreement establishes binding commitments by all parties to prepare, communicate and maintain a nationally determined contribution (NDC) and to pursue domestic measures to achieve them. It also prescribes that parties shall communicate their NDCs every 5 years and provide necessary information for clarity and transparency.
- Sinks and reservoirs: The parties have to conserve and enhance, as appropriate, sinks and reservoirs of GHG including forests.
- Adaptation: The agreement establishes a global goal on adaptation – of enhancing adaptive capacity, strengthening resilience and reducing vulnerability to climate change in the context of the temperature goal of the agreement.
- Loss & Damage: The agreement recognises the importance of averting, minimising and addressing loss

and damage associated with the adverse effects of climate change, including extreme weather events and slow onset events, and the role of sustainable development in reducing risk of loss and damage.

- Finance, technology and capacity building support: The Paris agreement reaffirms the obligations of developed countries to support the efforts of developing countries to build clean, climate resilient futures, while for first time encouraging voluntary contributions by other parties. It also provides for the financial mechanism of the convention, including the Green Climate Fund (GCF)
- Climate change education, training, public awareness, public participation and public access to information are also to be enhanced under the agreement.
- Transparency, implementation and compliance: The agreement relies on a robust transparency and accounting system to provide clarity on action and support by the parties, with flexibility for their differing capabilities.

The first Global stocktaking took place in 2023 during COP 28 in Dubai. There will be subsequent stocktaking every five years to assess the collective progress in achieving the goals.

COP 28 was particularly momentous as it marked the conclusion of the first 'global stock take' of the world's efforts to address climate change under the Paris Agreement. Having shown that progress was too slow across all areas of climate action, from reducing greenhouse gas emissions, to strengthening resilience to a changing climate, to getting the financial and technological support to vulnerable nations – countries responded with a decision on how to accelerate action across all areas by 2030. This includes a call on governments to speed up the transition away from fossil fuels to renewables such as wind and solar power in their next round of climate commitments.

COP 28 resulted in unprecedented recognition and momentum for linking efforts to address the climate and biodiversity crises. Alongside pollution, these constitute the triple planetary crisis—the three, main interlinked environmental issues facing humanity. Governments were called upon to consider ecosystems, biodiversity, and carbon stores, such as forests, when developing their stronger national climate action plans (known as nationally determined contributions)

(Source: https://unfccc.int)

Table 2: Sustainable Development Goals

(Source : https://sdgs.un.org/goals#icons)

United Nations has provided a brief narration with recent developments and factual figures in their website. Sustainability, being a vital topic and closely connected to ESG, has to be addressed in detail. United Nations' brief explanation on UN SDG is reproduced as below:

No Poverty: The first goal being No Poverty means to end Poverty in all its forms everywhere. In 2020, the number of people living in extreme poverty (living on less than US $ 2.15 a day) rose to 724 million. Those living in extreme poverty struggle to fulfil the most basic needs (health, education, access to water and sanitation). Recovery from the pandemic has been slow and uneven, with extreme poverty dropping from 9.3 % in 2020 to 8.8 % in 2021. The conflict in Ukraine has disrupted global trade, leading to increased living cost that are disproportionately impacting the poor. Furthermore, climate change poses substantial threats to poverty reduction. Data suggest that by the end of 2022, 8.4 % of world's population, or as many as 678 million people, could still be living in extreme poverty. Poverty affects developed countries as well. Almost 30 million children are growing up poor in the world's richest countries. Eradicating poverty in all its forms remains one of the greatest challenges facing humanity. While the number of people living in extreme poverty dropped by more than half between 1990 and 2015 – from 1.9 billion to 731 million – too many are still struggling for the most basic human needs. A surge in action and investment to enhance economic opportunities, improve education and extended social protection to all, particularly the most excluded, is crucial to delivering on the central commitment to end poverty and leave no one behind.

Zero Hunger: Zero hunger means to end hunger and to achieve food security and improved nutrition and promote sustainable agriculture. In 2022, about 9.2 per cent of the world population was facing chronic hunger, equivalent to about 735 million people - 122 million more than in 2019. Hunger and malnutrition are barriers to sustainable development because hungry people are less productive, more prone to disease, and less able to improve their livelihoods. To nourish today's 735 million hungry people and the additional 2 billion people expected by 2050, a profound change of the global food and agriculture system is needed. To achieve zero hunger by 2030, urgent coordinated action and policy solutions are imperative to address entrenched inequalities, transform food systems, invest in sustainable agricultural practices, and reduce and mitigate the impact of conflict and the pandemic on global nutrition and food security

Good Health and Well Being: Good health and well-being, ensures healthy lives and promote well-being for all at all ages. Great strides have been made in improving people's health in recent years. 146 out of 200 countries or areas have already met or are on track to meet the SDG target on under-5 mortality. Effective HIV treatment has cut global AIDS related deaths by 52 per cent since 2010 and at least one neglected tropical disease has been eliminated in 47 countries. However, inequalities in health care access still persist. The COVID-19 pandemic and other ongoing crises have impeded progress towards Goal 3. Childhood vaccinations have experienced the largest decline in three decades. Tuberculosis and malaria deaths have increased compared with pre-pandemic levels. The Sustainable Development Goals (SDGs) make a bold commitment to end the epidemics of AIDS, tuberculosis, malaria and other communicable diseases by 2030. The aim is to achieve universal health coverage and provide access to safe and affordable medicines and vaccines for all. To overcome these setbacks and address long-standing health care shortcomings, increased investment in health systems is needed to support countries in their recovery and build resilience against future health threats.

Quality Education: Quality education means ensuring inclusive and equitable quality education and promote lifelong learning opportunities for all. Progress towards quality education was already slower than required before the pandemic, but COVID-19 has had devastating impacts on education, causing learning losses in four out of five of the 104 countries studied. Without additional measures, an estimated 84 million children and young people will stay out of school and approximately 300 million students will lack the basic numeracy and literacy skills necessary for success in life. In addition to free primary and secondary schooling for all boys and girls by 2030, the aim is to provide equal access to affordable vocational training, eliminate gender and wealth disparities, and achieve universal access to quality higher education. Education is the key that will allow many other Sustainable Development Goals (SDGs) to be achieved. When people are able to get quality education they can break from the cycle of poverty. Education helps to reduce inequalities and to reach gender equality. It also empowers people everywhere to live more healthy and sustainable lives. Education is also crucial to fostering tolerance between people and contributes to more peaceful societies. To deliver this goal, education financing must become a national investment priority. Furthermore, measures such as making education free and compulsory, increasing the number of teachers, improving basic school infrastructure and embracing digital transformation are essential.

Gender Equality: Gender equality aims to achieve gender equality and empower all women and girls. Women and girls represent half of the world's population and therefore also half of its potential. But gender inequality persists everywhere and stagnates social progress. On average, women in the labour market still earn 23 percent less than men globally. On average, women spend about three times as many hours in unpaid domestic and care work as men. Sexual violence and exploitation, the unequal division of unpaid care and domestic work, and discrimination in public office, all remain huge barriers. All these areas of inequality have been exacerbated by the COVID-19 pandemic: there has been a surge in reports of sexual violence, women have taken on more care work due to school closures, and 70% of health and social workers globally are women. At the current rate, it will take an estimated 300 years to end child marriage, 286 years to close gaps in legal protection and remove discriminatory laws, 140 years for women to be represented equally in positions of power and leadership in the workplace, and 47 years to achieve equal representation in national parliaments. Political leadership, investments and comprehensive policy reforms are needed to dismantle systemic barriers to achieving Goal 5. Gender equality is a cross-cutting objective and must be a key focus of national policies, budgets and institutions. Gender equality is not only a fundamental human right, but a necessary foundation for a peaceful, prosperous and sustainable world.

Clean Water and Sanitation: This goal aims to ensure availability and sustainable management of water and sanitation for all. Access to water, sanitation and hygiene is a human right. Yet billions are still faced with daily challenges accessing even the most basic of services. Water scarcity is projected to increase with the rise of global temperatures as a result of climate change. In 2020, 2.4 billion people lived in water-stressed countries. In 2022, 2.2 billion people still lacked safely managed drinking water, including 703 million without a basic water service; 3.5 billion people lacked safely managed sanitation, including 1.5 billion without basic sanitation services; and 2 billion lacked a basic handwashing facility, including 653 million with no handwashing facility at all. There has been positive progress. Between 2015 and 2022, the proportion of the world's population with access to safely managed drinking water increased from 69 per cent to 73 per cent. Investments in infrastructure and sanitation facilities; protection and restoration of water-related ecosystems; and hygiene education are among the steps necessary to ensure universal access to safe and affordable drinking water for all by

2030. It's difficult to achieve this goal by 2030. To get back on track, key strategies include increasing sector-wide investment and capacity-building, promoting innovation and evidence-based action, enhancing cross-sectoral coordination and cooperation among all stakeholders, and adopting a more integrated and holistic approach to water management.

Affordable and Clean Energy: Affordable and clean energy ensures access to affordable, reliable, sustainable and modern energy for all. Our everyday life depends on reliable and affordable energy. And yet the consumption of energy is the dominant contributor to climate change, accounting for around 60 percent of total global greenhouse gas emissions. From 2015 to 2021, the proportion of the global population with access to electricity has increased from 87 per cent to 91 per cent. In 2021, developing countries installed a record-breaking 268 watts per capita of renewable energy-generating capacity. And yet, in 2021 there were still 675 million people around the world with no access to electricity. Ensuring universal access to affordable electricity by 2030 means investing in clean energy sources such as solar, wind and thermal. Expanding infrastructure and upgrading technology to provide clean energy in all developing countries is a crucial goal that can both encourage growth and help the environment. To ensure access to energy for all by 2030, we must accelerate electrification, increase investments in renewable energy, improve energy efficiency and develop enabling policies and regulatory frameworks.

Decent Work and Economic Growth: The objective of this goal is Promote sustained, inclusive and sustainable economic growth, full and productive employment and decent work for all. Multiple crises are placing the global economy under serious threat. Global real GDP per capita growth is forecast to slow down in 2023 and with ever increasing challenging economic conditions, more workers are turning to informal employment. Globally, labour productivity has increased, and the unemployment rate has decreased. However, more progress is needed to increase employment opportunities, especially for young people, reduce informal employment and labour market inequality (particularly in terms of the gender pay gap), promote safe and secure working environments, and improve access to financial services to ensure sustained and inclusive economic growth. The global unemployment rate declined significantly in 2022, falling to 5.4 per cent from a peak of 6.6 per cent in 2020 as economies began recovering from the shock of the COVID-19 pandemic. This rate was lower than the pre- pandemic level of 5.5 per cent in 2019. A persistent lack of decent work opportunities, insufficient investments and under-consumption contribute to the erosion of the basic social contract: that all must share in progress. The creation of quality jobs remains a major challenge for almost all economies. Achieving Goal 8 will require a wholesale reform of the financial system to tackle rising debts, economic uncertainty and trade tensions, while promoting equitable pay and decent work for young people

Industry, Innovation and Infrastructure: This goal aims to build resilient infrastructure, promote inclusive and sustainable industrialization and foster innovation. The manufacturing industry's recovery from COVID-19 is incomplete and uneven. Global manufacturing growth slowed down to 3.3 per cent in 2022, from 7.4 per cent in 2021. The share of manufacturing in Least Developed Countries (LDCs) remains low, posing a serious challenge to the target of doubling industry's share of GDP by 2030. However, medium- high and high-technology industries demonstrated robust growth rates. As of 2022, 95 per cent of the world's population was within reach of a mobile broadband network, but some areas remain underserved. Investments in infrastructure – transport, irrigation, energy and information and communication technology – are crucial to achieving sustainable development and empowering communities in many countries. To achieve this goal by 2030, it is also essential to support LDCs, invest in advanced technologies, lower carbon emissions and increase mobile broadband access.

Reduce Inequalities: The aim of this goal is to reduce inequality within and among countries. Inequality threatens long-term social and economic development, harms poverty reduction and destroys people's sense of fulfilment and self-worth. The incomes of the poorest 40 per cent of the population had been growing faster than the national average in most countries. But emerging yet inconclusive evidence suggests that COVID-19 may have put a dent in this positive trend of falling within-country inequality. The pandemic has caused the largest rise in between-country inequality in three decades. Reducing both within, and between country inequality requires equitable resource distribution, investing in education and skills development, implementing social protection measures, combating discrimination, supporting marginalized groups and fostering international cooperation for fair trade and financial systems.

Sustainable Cities and Communities: The objective of this goal is to make cities and human settlements inclusive, safe, resilient and sustainable. Half of the world's population live in cities. This is projected to reach 70 per cent by 2050. In the developing world, the rapid growth of cities, along with the increasing rural to urban migration, has led to a boom in mega-cities. In 1990, there were ten mega-cities with 10 million inhabitants or more. In 2014, there are 28 mega-cities, home to a total of 453 million people.

This rapid urbanization outpaces the development of housing, infrastructure and services, which led to a rise in slums or slum-like conditions. In 2020, an estimated 1.1 billion urban residents lived in slums or slum-like conditions. Over the next 30 years, an additional 2 billion people are expected to live in such settlements. Sustainable development cannot be achieved without significantly transforming the way urban spaces are built and managed. Making cities safe and sustainable means ensuring access to safe and affordable housing, upgrading slum settlements, investing in public transport, creating green spaces, and improving urban planning and management in a way that is both participatory and inclusive.

Responsible Consumption and Production: This goal ensure sustainable consumption and production patterns. If the global population reaches 9.8 billion by 2050, the equivalent of almost three planets will be required to provide the natural resources needed to sustain current lifestyles. Global crises triggered a resurgence in fossil fuel subsidies, nearly doubling from 2020 to 2021. In 2021, governments spent an estimated $732 billion on subsidies for coal, oil and gas, nearly doubling the $375 billion spent in 2020. In 2021, although 828 million people were facing hunger, 13.2 per cent of the world's food was lost after harvest along the supply chain from farm to consumer. The trend towards sustainability reporting is on the rise, with around 70 per cent of monitored companies publishing sustainability reports in 2021. In 2022, 67 national governments reported to the United Nations Environment Program on the implementation of sustainable public procurement policies and action plans, a 50 per cent increase from 2020. Support should be provided to developing countries to move towards more sustainable patterns of consumption by 2030.

Climate Action: This goal requires urgent action to combat climate change and its impacts. Climate change affects every country on every continent. It is caused by human activities and threatens the future of our planet. With rising greenhouse gas emissions, climate change is occurring at rates much faster than anticipated and its effects are clearly felt world- wide. The impacts include changing weather patterns, rising sea level, and more extreme weather events. If left unchecked, climate change will undo a lot of the progress made over the past years in development. It will also provoke mass migrations that will lead to instability and wars. Between 2010 and 2020, highly vulnerable regions, home to approximately 3.3–3.6 billion people, experienced 15 times higher human mortality rates from floods, droughts and storms compared to regions with very low vulnerability. Sea levels continued to rise in 2022, reaching a new record since satellite measurements in 1993. Affordable, scalable solutions are now available to enable countries to leapfrog to cleaner, more resilient, and low-carbon economies. Climate change is a global challenge that requires coordinated international cooperation.

Life below Water: The aim of this goal is to conserve and sustainably use the oceans, seas and marine resources for sustainable development. Oceans cover three-quarters of the Earth's surface, contain 97 percent of the Earth's water, and represent 99 percent of the living space on the planet by volume. The world's oceans provide key natural resources including food, medicines, biofuels and other products; help with the breakdown and removal of waste and pollution; and their coastal ecosystems act as buffers to reduce damage from storms. However, marine pollution is reaching alarming levels, with over 17 million metric tons clogging the ocean in 2021, a figure set to double or triple by 2040.

Currently, the ocean's average pH is 8.1, about 30 per cent more acidic than in pre-industrial times. Ocean acidification threatens the survival of marine life, disrupts the food web, and undermines vital services provided by the ocean and our own food security. Careful management of this essential global resource is a key feature of a sustainable future. This includes increasing funding for ocean science, intensifying conservation efforts, and urgently turning the tide on climate change to safeguard the planet's largest ecosystem.

Life on Land: Life on land aims to Protect, restore and promote sustainable use of terrestrial ecosystems, sustainably manage forests, combat desertification, halt and reverse land degradation, and halt biodiversity loss. Terrestrial ecosystems are vital for sustaining human life, contributing to over half of global GDP and encompassing diverse cultural, spiritual, and economic values. Global forest coverage decreased from 31.9 per cent in 2000 (4.2 billion hectares) to 31.2 per cent (4.1 billion hectares) in 2020. In 2021, Official Development Assistance (ODA) in support of biodiversity increased by 26.2 per cent from $7.7 billion in 2020 to $9.8 billion. In 2022, 21 per cent of reptile species are threatened. Between 2015 and 2019, at least 100 million hectares of healthy and productive land were degraded every year, impacting the lives of 1.3 billion people. Halting deforestation and restoring the use of terrestrial ecosystems is necessary to reduce the loss of natural habitats and biodiversity which are part of our common heritage.

Peace, Justice and Strong Institutions: This goal aims to promote peaceful and inclusive societies for sustainable development, provide access to justice for all and build effective, accountable and inclusive institutions at all levels. People everywhere should be free of fear from all forms of violence and feel safe as they go about their lives whatever their ethnicity, faith or sexual orientation. Civilian deaths directly related to 12 of the world's deadliest conflicts increased by 53 per cent between 2021 and 2022, marking the first rise since the adoption of the 2030 Agenda in 2015. The year 2022 witnessed a more than 50 per cent increase in conflict-related civilian deaths. High levels of armed violence and insecurity have a destructive impact on a country's development. Sexual violence, crime, exploitation and torture are prevalent where there is conflict or no rule of law, and countries must take measures to protect those who are most at risk. By the end of 2022, 108.4 million people were forcibly displaced worldwide – an increase of 19 million compared with the end of 2021 and two and a half times the number of a decade ago. In 2021, there were approximately 458,000 intentional homicides – the highest number in the past two decades. Governments, civil society and communities need to work together to find lasting solutions to conflict and insecurity. Strengthening the rule of law and promoting human rights is key to this process, as is reducing the flow of illicit arms, combating corruption, and ensuring inclusive participation at all times.

Partnership for the Goals: The aim of this goal is to strengthen the means of implementation and revitalize the global partnership for sustainable development. The 2030 Agenda for Sustainable Development is universal and calls for action by all countries – developed and developing – to ensure no one is left behind. It requires partnerships between governments, the private sector, and civil society. The Sustainable Development Goals can only be realized with a strong commitment to global partnership and cooperation. The total external debt of low- and middle-income countries reached $9 trillion in 2021, recording a 5.6 per cent increase from 2020. In 2022, global exports increased sharply by

12.3 per cent, and global trade reached a record $32 trillion. In 2022, net ODA (**Official Development Assistance**) flows by member countries of the Development Assistance Committee (DAC) reached $206 billion. To be successful, everyone needs to mobilize both existing and additional resources, and developed countries will need to fulfil their official development assistance commitments.

(Source : https://www.un.org)

SOCIAL: HALLMARKS OF A CIVILIZED SOCIETY

The main characteristic of a civilized society is social equality. There cannot be any discrimination with respect to race, religion, sex, color, nationality, language, etc., in a civilized society.

Being responsible corporate citizens, corporates should have various policies to achieve social equality. Below are a few examples:

- DEI policy
- Human Rights policy
- Health & Safety Policy
- Fair pay and living wages
- Equal employment opportunities
- Opportunity for learning and development
- Rural transformation
- Restoration of heritage

GOVERNANCE

According to World Economic forum, (document titled - Defining the 'G 'in ESG published in June 2022) corporate governance includes factors as per table below.

Table 3: Factors included in corporate governance - Defining 'G' in ESG, by WEF

Factors	Example: Sub factors, key indicators
Business ethics	Purpose, value, culture, integrity beyond compliance, ESG integration, pursuit of and reporting on KPIs
Board composition	Competencies, diversity, structure, committees, oversight capacity, independence
Corporate leadership	Tone, knowledge, experience, power allocation, compensation, decision-making process, independence, and empowerment of compliance function.
Risk and crisis management	Preparedness, mitigation, past performance, regulatory compliance, segregation of duties, audit independence, shareholder rights, information governance, cyber security
Resource allocation	Capital allocation, personnel allocation, mergers and acquisition
Incentive structures	Compensation, promotion, reporting structures, defined prohibited misconduct, disciplinary measures.
Political responsibility	Lobbying, amicus briefs, campaign finance, political contribution
Transparency	Ownership, subsidiaries / holdings, open contracting, lobbying, charitable donations, countries of operation, verifiability of disclosures
Anti-corruption and integrity	Training and communications, whistle–blower protocols, due diligence, risk assessments, public procurement, government relations, gifts and entertainment, conflict of interest, remuneration and payment procedures, record keeping, financial controls, reporting and accounting, contractual obligations, public commitments, past incidents, internal investigation and remediation
Tax strategy	Tax compliance, anti-tax avoidance, tax disclosures
Fair competitive practices	Anti-collusion, anti-exclusion, anti-monopoly, anti-coercion, market-based pricing
Stakeholder engagement	Understanding corporate impact and stakeholder priorities, pursuing stakeholder-centered practices
Supply/value chain management	ESG integration, transparency, contractual obligations, countries of operation

(Source: World Economic Forum)

Building on the above foundational concepts of Environment, Social, and Governance (ESG), we now turn our attention to a critical discussion: the Calibration Paradox within ESG. This paradox highlights the complexities inherent in aligning diverse stakeholder interests, standards, and measurement frameworks. Accordingly, it underscores the urgent need for an innovative approach—a new calibrator, which we introduce as the ESG Quanta Calibrator.

Environmental, Social, and Governance (ESG) ratings were created to bring clarity to sustainable investing. Instead, they have produced a paradox. The same company, evaluated by different ESG rating agencies, often receives materially different scores, sometimes even opposite assessments. For investors, regulators, and corporate leaders, this inconsistency has transformed ESG from a guiding framework into a source of confusion.

This phenomenon is not a marginal flaw. It is systemic. ESG ratings influence capital allocation, cost of capital, index inclusion, executive compensation, and corporate strategy. When those ratings lack calibration, markets misprice risk, companies misallocate resources, and sustainability efforts lose credibility.

This book defines this systemic inconsistency as the **Calibration Paradox**: the absence of a common reference framework that allows ESG assessments to be comparable, interoperable, and decision useful. While diversity of perspective is valuable, the absence of calibration turns pluralism into noise.

Over the past two decades, ESG has evolved rapidly. Governments have embedded sustainability into regulation, investors have integrated ESG into portfolio construction, and corporations now publish extensive non-financial disclosures. Yet the mechanisms that translate this information into ratings remain fragmented.

Differences in scope, data sources, measurement techniques, and weighting structures have created a landscape where ESG scores often reflect the methodology of the rater more than the sustainability performance of the rated entity.

This book argues that ESG does not suffer from a lack of data, intention, or institutional support. It suffers from a lack of calibration.

To address this gap, the book introduces the **ESG Quanta Calibrator**, a new global ESG rating framework designed to normalize divergent ESG assessments without erasing sectoral nuance or materiality. Rather than replacing existing ESG ratings, the Quanta Calibrator functions as a meta-calibration layer, enabling comparability, transparency, and interpretive coherence across rating systems.

Through a combination of theoretical grounding, empirical analysis, and applied case studies, this work demonstrates how calibrated ESG assessments can restore trust, improve capital efficiency, and align sustainability measurement with real-world impact.

The objective is not to simplify ESG, but to make it intelligible.

PART ONE
THE BROKEN ESG RATING WORLD

CHAPTER 1
WHEN ONE COMPANY HAS MANY TRUTHS

HOW THE SAME FIRM RECEIVES CONTRADICTORY ESG SCORES

In traditional financial markets, the valuation of a company may vary across analysts, but the underlying financial statements remain common and standardized. ESG assessment operates very differently. A single company can simultaneously be classified as a sustainability leader by one ESG rating agency and a laggard by another. These contradictions are not rare exceptions; they are a defining characteristic of the current ESG rating landscape.

This phenomenon has been documented repeatedly across markets and sectors. Studies comparing leading ESG rating providers consistently show low correlation between ESG scores assigned to the same firm. In some cases, correlation coefficients between major agencies fall below levels that would be considered acceptable for traditional credit ratings or financial risk metrics. The result is a fragmented sustainability signal that complicates interpretation and weakens confidence.

For investors, this divergence creates practical dilemmas. Portfolio construction based on one ESG dataset may lead to materially different asset allocations than portfolios built using another dataset. Fund performance, perceived sustainability alignment, and even regulatory compliance can vary depending solely on the choice of ESG rating provider. ESG integration, therefore, becomes less a matter of sustainability conviction and more a function of data vendor selection.

Corporates face an equally complex challenge. Companies investing heavily in sustainability initiatives may find their efforts rewarded by one rating agency and overlooked or penalized by another. This inconsistency undermines internal alignment, weakens the business case for long-term sustainability investments, and increases the risk of strategic fatigue. In extreme cases, firms may optimize disclosures to satisfy specific rating methodologies rather than improve underlying sustainability performance.

Regulators and policymakers are not immune to these effects. As ESG metrics increasingly inform disclosure mandates, taxonomy alignment, and prudential regulation, inconsistent ratings threaten to compromise policy effectiveness. Without calibration, ESG-based regulation risks embedding methodological bias rather than objective sustainability assessment.

The existence of multiple ESG perspectives is not inherently problematic. Sustainability is multidimensional, context specific, and value-laden. However, the absence of a calibration mechanism that translates diverse assessments into a coherent reference framework is a structural flaw. Without calibration, ESG ratings cannot reliably fulfil their core function: enabling informed, comparable, and forward-looking decision-making.

This chapter establishes the empirical reality of ESG divergence and frames it not as a data quality issue, but as a systems design problem. Understanding this distinction is essential before exploring why existing methodologies fail and how a calibrated solution can emerge.

According to Larry Swedroe in his article titled – "Do wide divergences in ESG ratings doom investors "published in www.advisorperspectives.com (20th June 2021) makes comparison of ESG rating by three different agencies for six different companies. The result is not uniform. The reason includes difference in valuation approach, weightage given to environment, social and governance by different agencies are different and varying from industry to industry etc. In the below chart environmental factor for Facebook is 1 percentile by Sustainalytics and 96 percentiles by MSCI.

Table 4: Comparison of ESG rating by 3 different agencies for six different companies

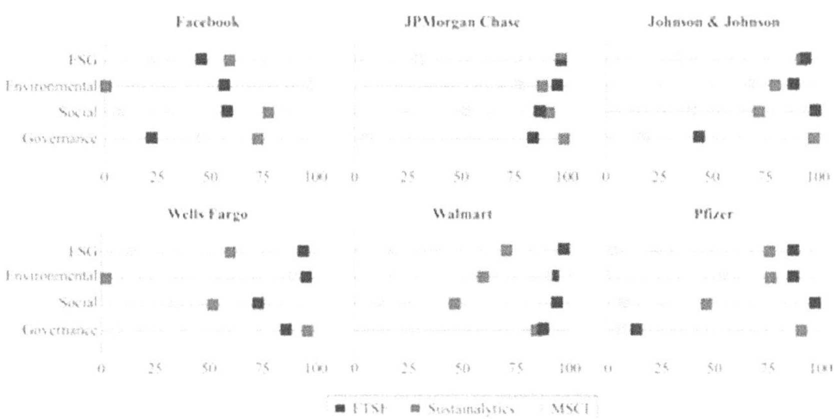

(Source : Data from MSCI , FTSE Russell and Sustainalytics)

In the above study Six company's ESG ratings by Three agencies were analysed. The Companies are:

- Facebook
- JP Morgan Chase
- Johnson & Johnson
- Wells Fargo
- Walmart
- Pfizer

The Three rating agencies are :

- FTSE (Financial Times Stock Exchange) Russell ESG Rating
- MSCI (Morgan Stanley Capital International) ESG ratings
- Sustainalytics

Let's evaluate the cases of the above companies:

1. Facebook

Environment score given by M/s Sustainalytics is almost zero (minimum) , whereas M/s MSCI is close to 100 (maximum) and M/s FTSE gave slightly over 50, which is the midway. When it comes to the score for social element, MSCI gave low score whereas Sustainalytics gave higher score which is above 75 and FTSE gave slightly high than 50. For Governance element FTSE gave close to 25, whereas MSCI and Sustainalytics's scores were close to 50 and 75 respectively. Considering the overall ESG score MSCI and FTSE gave less than 25 and 50 respectively , whereas Sustainalytics gave higher than 50 . So to conclude the case of M/s

Facebook , all the three rating agencies gave scores with wide variance.

2. JP Morgan Chase

Environment score given by M/s Sustainalytics , M/s FTSE and M/s MSCI are in between 75 and 100, which shows some similarity. For social element, Sustainalytics and FTSE gave scores in between 75 and 100, whereas MSCI gave only close to 50. Governance element 's score also is almost in line with social score for Sustainalytics and FTSE. Sustainalytics and FTSE gave scores in between 75 and 100, whereas MCSI score is very low – close to minimum. The consolidated ESG score given by Sustainalytics and FTSE are similar whereas MSCI is close to 25. On an overall analysis Sustainalytics and FTSE gave almost similar scores , whereas MCSI gave lesser score compared to others. So to conclude the case of M/s JP Morgan Chase , FTSE and Sustainalytics gave similar score , without much variation. But MSCI's scores are much lower than the other two rating agencies.

3. Johnson & Johnson

Environment score given by M/s Sustainalytics and M/s FTSE is between 75 and 100, whereas MSCI is between 50 and 75. For social element, the scores awarded by three agencies have wide variations viz FTSE gave scores close to 100, Sustainalytics gave slightly less than 75 and MSCI awarded between 25 and 50. Governance element 's score has wide variance : MSCI is less than 25 , FTSE is slightly less than 50 and Sustainalytics is close to 100. But the overall ESG score awarded by Sustainalytics and FTSE are similar (between 75 and 100) , whereas MSCI is between 25 and 50. So the analysis in the case of M/s Johnson C Johnson is MSCI's score is much lesser than other two rating agencies, even though there are variations in FTSE and Sustainalytics 's score but not so wide as MSCI.

4. Wells Fargo

Environment score given by M/s MSCI and M/s FTSE is close to 100, whereas Sustainalytics is close to minimum. For social element, the scores awarded by three agencies have no similarity, MSCI between 25 and 50 , Sustainalytics – slightly above 50 and FTSE – close to 75. Governance element 's score by FTSE and Sustainalytics are almost equal (between 75 and 100) , whereas MSCI is close to minimum. The overall ESG score awarded by MSCI is less than 25 , Sustainalytics is slightly higher than 50 and FTSE close to maximum. So , to conclude ,almost all the individual elements and consolidated score have wide variance.

5. Walmart

Environment score given by M/s MSCI and M/s FTSE is close to 100, whereas Sustainalytics is slightly higher than 50. For social element, the scores awarded by three agencies have no similarity, MSCI is close to minimum , Sustainalytics – slightly less than 50 and FTSE – close to 100. Governance element 's score by FTSE and Sustainalytics are almost equal (between 75 and 100) , whereas MSCI is close to 25. The overall ESG score awarded by MSCI is less than 25 , Sustainalytics is close to 75 and FTSE close to maximum. So , to conclude ,almost all the three elements and consolidated score have wide variance .

6. Pfizer

Environment score given by M/s Sustainalytics and FTSE is between 75 and 100, whereas M/s MSCI is close to 50. When it comes to the score for social element, MSCI gave low score whereas Sustainalytics is on the midway , close to 50 and FTSE gave close to 100. For Governance element FTSE and MSCI gave very less - whereas Sustainalytics's gave a higher score close to 100. Considering the overall ESG score MSCI gave less than 25 (close to minimum) , whereas Sustainalytics gave close to 75 and FTSE higher than 75 . So to conclude the case of M/s Pfizer , all the three rating agencies gave scores with wide variance.

A significant contributor to methodological inconsistency stems from the mergers and acquisitions among ESG rating agencies. When a company is rated by an agency that subsequently adopts a different methodology following a merger, the resulting score may diverge substantially from previous assessments. This can lead to confusion among investors and stakeholders, who rely on these ratings for informed decision-making.

Furthermore, the non-financial nature of most ESG criteria means that pertinent information is often absent from standard company disclosures, media reports, and regulatory filings. For multinational corporations operating across numerous jurisdictions, negative factors present in specific countries may not be reflected in consolidated reports, potentially leading to inaccurate or misleading overall scores. Such misrepresentations pose a risk to various stakeholders, including investors, employees, and customers, who depend on accurate ESG assessments.

The findings highlight that existing ESG rating agencies tend to priorities transaction-based evaluation over a holistic assessment of the company's internal systems. Relying solely on transaction analysis is insufficient for establishing effective professional management and governance structures. To foster true professionalism and sustainable management, organisations must implement robust systems that are diligently managed, responsive to deviations, and adaptable to technological and situational changes. Moreover, it is essential to ensure that comprehensive education and communication are provided to all stakeholders involved.

In summary, the current landscape of ESG ratings is characterized by significant methodological inconsistencies and transparency concerns. Addressing these challenges requires a shift towards more standardised, system-oriented evaluation frameworks, greater disclosure of processes and data volumes, and a commitment to continuous improvement and stakeholder engagement. Only through such measures can ESG ratings serve as a reliable tool for assessing corporate responsibility and guiding investment decisions.

CHAPTER 2
WHY ESG RATINGS MATTER MORE THAN EVER

CAPITAL FLOWS, REGULATION, REPUTATION, AND RISK

ESG ratings were once considered peripheral tools, useful mainly for niche ethical investors and exclusionary screening strategies. That era has ended. Today, ESG ratings sit at the intersection of capital markets, corporate governance, public policy, and societal expectations. Their influence has expanded rapidly, often faster than the methodological maturity required to support that influence.

Institutional investors now rely on ESG ratings to guide portfolio construction, risk management, and stewardship decisions. Pension funds, sovereign wealth funds, insurance companies, and asset managers integrate ESG scores into investment mandates that control trillions of dollars in capital. In many cases, ESG ratings directly affect asset allocation, index inclusion, and fund eligibility. A shift in ESG score can trigger capital inflows or outflows that rival traditional financial events.

Beyond investment decisions, ESG ratings increasingly shape the cost of capital. Lenders and bond investors use ESG metrics to price risk, determine covenants, and assess long-term resilience. Sustainability-linked loans and bonds explicitly tie financing costs to ESG performance indicators, embedding ESG scores into contractual financial outcomes. In this context, an inconsistent or poorly calibrated ESG rating does not merely distort perception; it alters economic reality.

Corporate behavior has evolved in response to this expanding influence. Boards now review ESG ratings alongside financial performance. Executive compensation structures incorporate ESG-linked key performance indicators. Sustainability teams design disclosure strategies with rating agency methodologies in mind. While this reflects progress in elevating sustainability to the strategic level, it also exposes firms to methodological dependency. Companies may prioritize actions that improve specific ESG scores rather than those that generate genuine long- term impact.

Regulators have further amplified the importance of ESG ratings. Disclosure regimes, sustainable finance taxonomies, and prudential regulations increasingly reference ESG concepts, metrics, and classifications. In some jurisdictions, ESG ratings inform supervisory assessments and regulatory expectations. When regulatory frameworks implicitly or explicitly rely on ESG ratings, inconsistencies between rating systems risk translating into regulatory inconsistency.

Public perception and reputational dynamics add another layer of significance. ESG ratings influence how companies are perceived by customers, employees, civil society, and the media. A downgrade can attract public scrutiny, activist pressure, or litigation risk. Conversely, favorable ESG ratings can enhance brand equity and social license to operate. These reputational effects often materialize faster than financial ones, amplifying the impact of ESG assessments.

The cumulative result is that ESG ratings now function as a form of informal infrastructure within global capitalism. They shape incentives, expectations, and behavior across markets and institutions. Yet unlike traditional financial infrastructure, ESG ratings lack standardized calibration, common reference points, and universally accepted interpretive rules.

This asymmetry between influence and methodological coherence is the core risk. As ESG ratings matter more than ever, their inconsistencies matter more too. Without calibration, the growing reliance on ESG ratings threatens to undermine the very objectives they were designed to advance: efficient capital allocation, responsible corporate behavior, and credible sustainability transitions.

This chapter establishes why ESG ratings cannot be treated as soft or supplementary metrics. They are consequential instruments of economic governance.

Companies excelling in the management of ESG issues can enhance shareholder value, whether by prudently managing risks, anticipating regulatory actions, or accessing new markets, while simultaneously advancing the sustainable development of the societies in which they operate. Furthermore, the handling of ESG matters often significantly influences a company's reputation and branding, adding value in ways that extend beyond balance sheets. Ultimately, successful investment is inextricably linked to a vibrant economy, a condition dependent upon a healthy civil society, which itself relies on a sustainable planet. In the long view, investment markets have an unmistakable self-interest in fostering better management of environmental and social impacts, thereby contributing to the sustainable progress of the global community. A more comprehensive integration of environmental, social and governance (ESG) considerations in investment decisions is anticipated to yield greater market stability and predictability. ESG functions as a transformative force with a long-term horizon. Expecting immediate results from ESG initiatives is, at best, immature and unrealistic; it is in the long term that the true benefits of ESG materialise. The case of the FMCG giant M/s Unilever stands as a classic illustration.

By embedding sustainability at the core of its operations over a period of ten to twenty years, M/s Unilever realised savings of $1.27 billion across its functions. This achievement was made possible by prioritising sustainable sourcing and actively addressing the risks posed by climate change. The company's growth was driven by the introduction of its Sustainable Living Brands, which were defined by a strong social and environmental mission. (Source: Mr. Alan Jope 's , Ex. CEO Unilever - Interview.)

Sustainable growth is best defined as development that satisfies the needs of the present without compromising the ability of future generations to meet their own needs. This approach encompasses not only environmental and social dimensions but also economic progress. The United Nations Sustainable Development Goals (UN SDG) represent a strategic and comprehensive move towards achieving such growth.

Most of the governments realised the need for and importance of the ideology and passed various enactments for the implementation of ESG ideology. This initiative has a rampant growth which is visible now. Majority of fortune 500 companies publishes ESG report along with their annual report.

The chapters that follow examine why existing ESG frameworks struggle to meet this responsibility and why calibration is no longer optional, but essential.

CHAPTER 3
THE CALIBRATION PARADOX DEFINED

METHODOLOGICAL FRAGMENTATION, DATA ASYMMETRY, AND WEIGHT DISTORTION

The defining weakness of contemporary ESG ratings is not the absence of data, intent, or analytical sophistication. It is the absence of calibration. ESG ratings operate within parallel methodological universes, each internally coherent yet externally incompatible. The result is a paradox in which increasing analytical effort produces decreasing clarity.

This book defines this condition as the **Calibration Paradox**: a structural failure arising from the lack of a shared reference framework that allows ESG assessments generated by different methodologies to be compared, reconciled, and interpreted consistently. In the absence of calibration, ESG ratings reflect methodological preference more than underlying sustainability performance.

At the heart of the Calibration Paradox lies fragmentation. ESG rating agencies differ across multiple dimensions simultaneously. They apply different definitions of materiality, rely on divergent data sources, select distinct indicators, and assign varying weights to environmental, social, and governance factors. Some prioritize risk to the firm; others impact on society. Some emphasize disclosure quality, others outcome metrics. Each approach is defensible in isolation, yet collectively they generate incoherence.

This fragmentation is often misinterpreted as healthy diversity. While pluralism is valuable in sustainability analysis, pluralism without translation mechanisms becomes noise. Financial markets tolerate analytical diversity because shared accounting standards, calibrated benchmarks, and common risk metrics provide interpretive anchors. ESG lacks such anchors. Without calibration, diversity does not converge toward insight.

Data asymmetry further intensifies the paradox. ESG ratings increasingly rely on vast datasets sourced from corporate disclosures, third-party providers, media analysis etc. More data, however, has not produced greater alignment. Instead, it has expanded the surface area for divergence. Differences in data validation, estimation techniques, and treatment of missing information amplify score dispersion rather than reduce it.

Weighting structures introduce another layer of distortion. ESG ratings implicitly embed value judgments about what matters most. Environmental performance may dominate one rating, while governance practices dominate another. Sector-specific adjustments vary widely, as do assumptions about time horizons and transition pathways. These weighting decisions are rarely transparent to end users, yet they exert decisive influence over final scores.

The consequences of the Calibration Paradox extend beyond analytical inconvenience. Investors face inconsistent signals that complicate risk assessment and capital allocation. Corporates encounter conflicting incentives that dilute strategic focus. Regulators risk embedding methodological bias into policy frameworks. Over time, the credibility of ESG itself is weakened as stakeholders struggle to reconcile competing assessments.

Crucially, the Calibration Paradox cannot be resolved by standardization alone. Attempts to impose a single global ESG methodology risk oversimplification, political contestation, and loss of contextual nuance. Sustainability is inherently multidimensional and context dependent. The objective is not uniformity of assessment, but coherence of interpretation.

Calibration offers a different solution. Rather than replacing existing ESG methodologies, calibration establishes a meta-level reference framework that translates diverse assessments into a common interpretive space. It preserves methodological plurality while enabling comparability, convergence analysis, and decision usefulness.

The need of developing **ESG QUANTA CALIBRATOR** arises from variances in ESG ratings assigned by various rating agencies to the same company. An in-depth study reveals that there are major and minor variations in the rating of the three elements (E, S & G) individually and in the consolidated score. ESG does not have a uniform reporting standard globally, which renders comparison confusing and difficult.

The questions raised in during this study are as follows:

- What are the scoring criteria to be considered and evaluated?
- Which are the best data sources
- How should the system be evaluated in relation to policy creation, implementation, corrective action, periodic upgrades, and updating in response to technological advancement and contingencies?
- How is the ESG score related to business activities in different geographies?
- How can a justifiable index or weightage be identified?
- How does the score relate to financial or business volume?

This chapter reframes ESG divergence as a design flaw rather than a temporary market imperfection. Recognizing the Calibration Paradox is the necessary precondition for solving it. The chapters that follow examine why existing ESG frameworks struggle to overcome this paradox and lay the groundwork for a calibrated alternative.

PART TWO
WHY EXISTING FRAMEWORKS FAIL

CHAPTER 4
INSIDE ESG RATING METHODOLOGIES

WHAT RATING AGENCIES ACTUALLY MEASURE

To understand why ESG ratings diverge so sharply, it is necessary to examine how they are constructed. Despite superficial similarities in structure and terminology, ESG rating methodologies differ fundamentally in purpose, architecture, and interpretation. These differences are not always visible to end users, yet they decisively shape outcomes.

Most ESG rating systems follow a multi-stage process: data collection, indicator selection, scoring, weighting, and aggregation. Divergence emerges at each of these stages.

The first point of divergence is **data sourcing**. ESG rating agencies rely on varying combinations of corporate disclosures, questionnaires, third-party databases, media screening, NGO reports, satellite data, and algorithmic estimations. Some prioritize company-reported information, while others emphasize external controversy data. The treatment of missing, outdated, or unverifiable data varies widely, leading to structural inconsistencies before scoring even begins.

The second divergence lies in **indicator selection**. ESG is not a fixed dataset but a conceptual framework. Rating agencies decide which indicators represent environmental, social, and governance performance, often guided by proprietary materiality models. One methodology may emphasize carbon intensity and climate transition risk, while another prioritizes biodiversity, labor practices, or board independence. These choices reflect normative assumptions about what sustainability means.

Materiality frameworks further differentiate methodologies. Some ESG ratings adopt a financial materiality lens, focusing on risks and opportunities that affect enterprise value. Others apply a double materiality approach, incorporating impacts on society and the environment regardless of immediate financial relevance. While both perspectives are legitimate, their coexistence without calibration guarantees divergent results.

Scoring models introduce additional variation. Raw data may be normalized using peer benchmarking, absolute thresholds, trend analysis, or qualitative judgment. Performance may be assessed relative to industry peers or against global targets. Small methodological choices, such as how outliers are treated or how controversies decay over time, can materially alter scores.

Weighting and aggregation represent perhaps the most consequential and least transparent stage. Agencies assign weights to indicators, themes, and pillars based on internal logic that is rarely fully disclosed. Environmental, social, and governance components may carry different relative importance across sectors and regions. Aggregation methods may allow strong performance in one area to offset weak performance in another, or they may penalize poor performance asymmetrically.

These methodological choices are not errors. They are expressions of analytical judgment. The problem arises because they are embedded within opaque systems presented as objective scores. End users often interpret ESG ratings as definitive assessments rather than methodological outputs conditioned by specific assumptions.

Attempts to compare ESG ratings across providers frequently overlook this structural reality. Low correlation between scores is not a failure of execution but a predictable consequence of uncalibrated design. Without a common reference framework, each methodology produces its own internally consistent truth.

This chapter underscores a central insight: ESG rating divergence is not accidental. It is engineered through cumulative methodological choices made without calibration constraints. Recognizing this is essential before exploring why existing frameworks struggle to resolve divergence and how a calibrated meta-framework can reconcile plurality with coherence.

Major ESG Rating Agencies and Their Methodology

The prominent ESG rating agencies include:

- Bloomberg ESG Ratings
- MSCI (Morgan Stanley Capital International) ESG ratings
- Sustainalytics ESG risk ratings
- ISS (Institutional Shareholder Services) ESG Rating C Ranking
- Standard & Poor (S&P) Global

- Moody's ESG Score (VIGEO – EIRIS)
- CDP Scores (Formerly Carbon Disclosure Project)
- FTSE (Financial Times Stock Exchange) Russell ESG Rating
- Refinitiv ESG Scores
- Reprisk ESG Rating (RRR)
- Thomson Reuters ESG Research Data
- Dow Jones Sustainability Index (DJSI)
- Corporate Knights Global 100
- Ecovadis

Bloomberg ESG Ratings: Launched in 2008 after the acquisition of New Energy Finance, is a service that provides information on the environmental, social, and governance (ESG) performance of over 10,000 publicly listed companies globally. The service evaluates companies annually by collecting public ESG information disclosed by companies through corporate social responsibility (CSR) or sustainability reports, annual reports, websites, and other public sources, as well as through direct contact with the companies. The data is checked and standardized, including 120 indicators for environmental, social, and governance, such as carbon emissions, climate change impact, pollution, waste disposal, renewable energy, resource depletion, supply chain, political contributions, discrimination, diversity, community relations, human rights, cumulative voting, executive compensation, shareholder rights, takeover defence, staggered boards, and independent directors. The rating scale ranges from 0 to 100, with scores from third-party rating agencies such as RobecoSam, Sustainalytics, ISS Quality Score, and CDP Climate Disclosure Score, as well as an overview of historical ESG performance relative to peers. Bloomberg ESG Ratings focuses on mid-to large-cap companies with a market cap of more than $2 billion.

MSCI (Morgan Stanley Capital International) ESG Rating : MSCI ESG Rating provides a comprehensive evaluation of a company's environmental, social, and governance performance. MSCI ESG Research is one of the largest independent providers of ESG ratings, providing ESG ratings for over 6,000 global companies and more than 400,000 equity and fixed-income securities. The ratings are based on a scale of AAA-CCC and are updated every week. MSCI ESG Research looks at 37 key ESG issues, divided into three pillars (environmental, social, and governance) and ten themes. The data is collected from various sources such as government databases, company disclosures, and macro data from academic, government, and NGO databases. Companies are systematically monitored and reviewed, and new information is reflected in updates in reports weekly. In-depth company reviews occur at least annually. Companies are also invited to participate in a formal data verification process before the publication of their ESG Ratings report. The ratings are available through subscription-based access to reports . MSCI is currently consulting on whether ESG factors should be reflected in the MSCI GIMI (Global Investable Market Indices), which would likely mean that MSCI's ESG research would be integrated into the MSCI GIMI methodology.

Sustainalytics: Sustainalytics is a leading provider of ESG research and data, which helps investors identify and manage the risks and opportunities of investing in companies based on their environmental, social, and governance practices. The rating scale used by Sustainalytics is a score out of 100, which is based on a sector/industry comparison. The methodology used involves analysing key ESG issues and indicators, which are split into three themes: environmental, social, and governance. The set of issues and indicators analysed will vary by industry, with a specific weight placed on each issue. Sustainalytics covers at least 70 indicators in each industry. The ESG indicators are split into three dimensions: preparedness, disclosure, and performance. The company's ESG rating report is based on a quantitative and qualitative assessment of the company's performance and considers the company's management systems and policies, as well as their level of transparency and controversial incidents they may have been involved in.

ISS (Institutional Shareholder Services): ISS offers a range of ESG solutions to assist institutional investors in integrating responsible investment policies and practices into their investment decisions, engaging with companies, and executing their policies through voting. In 2015, ISS acquired Ethix SRI Advisors and formed a strategic partnership with RepRisk, allowing ISS to expand its ESG and socially responsible investing (SRI) research. ISS also provides climate change data and analytics from its acquisition of Climate Neutral Investments. ISS Quality Score offers in-depth research on corporate governance for over 5,600 publicly traded companies globally. The ISS Quality Score rating scale is based on a 1st to 10th decile, with a score in the 1st decile indicating relatively higher quality governance practices and lower governance risk, while a score in the 10th decile indicates relatively higher governance risk. The methodology analyses over 200 factors, divided into four pillars: board structure, compensation/remuneration, shareholder rights, and audit & risk oversight. A specific weight is placed on each factor depending on the governance standards in each region, the ISS voting policy, and the impact on governance practices. ISS-Ethix provides research, screening, and analysis on various ESG topics such as controversial weapons screening, ethical screens, energy & extractives screening, global sanctions screening, and research on companys' adherence to human rights, labour standards, environmental protection, and anti-corruption.

S&P (Standard & Poor) Global ESG Score: S&P Global ESG Scores are a measure of a company's exposure to and performance on key environmental, social, and governance (ESG) risks and opportunities. The scores focus on quantitative, performance driven metrics, as well as management programs and policies . The scores are measured on a scale of 0 – 100, where 100 represents the maximum score. Points are awarded based on the availability, quality, relevance, and performance of data points on ESG topics. These scores are constructed through the annual SCP Global Corporate Sustainability Assessment (CSA), which invites all companies in the research universe to participate. Companies submit responses and supporting evidence through an online portal and the data is assessed based on the latest financial year reporting. The scores and underlying data levels are updated monthly to reflect changes that may result from ongoing research processes. The CSA evaluates corporate sustainability risks, opportunities, and stakeholder impacts over the short, medium, and long term, with general criteria and industry specific factors being assessed. The questions within each criterion are structured to assess a company's awareness of the relevance and impact, quantification of risk exposure and potential opportunities, and implementation of strategies to manage sustainability risks and capitalize on opportunities.

Moody's ESG (VIGEO-EIRIS): Moody's ESG assessments measure the degree to which companies manage environmental, social, and governance (ESG) factors that affect their financial performance and how their business impacts the environments and societies in which they operate. The assessments are based on double materiality, meaning they include external environmental and social risks to financial performance, as well as how the company's operations impact its surroundings. Moody's ESG Solutions has adopted a revised version of the methodology. The key revisions to the current methodology include the introduction of an appendix that provides more details on the credit implications for financial institutions of E, S, and G considerations and how Moody's assigns IPSs (issuer profile scores) and CISs (credit impact scores). The assessment of a financial institution's exposure to ESG risks and benefits is primarily qualitative, and the methodology describes relevant considerations generally applicable across financial institution sectors. Additionally, a compendia document appendix will be introduced that provides more details on the qualitative considerations and illustrative types of quantitative metrics informing IPSs and CISs for financial institutions. Moody's may expand this compendium to provide further details of more sector specific considerations and types of metrics as more data become available or indicators become relevant to their analysis. Moody's expects no changes to outstanding ratings for financial institutions.

CDP : Formerly known as the Carbon Disclosure Project, is a scoring system that works to motivate companies to disclose and take action to reduce their environmental impacts. CDP uses its scoring methodology to incentivize companies to measure and manage environmental impacts through participation in CDP's Climate Change, Water, Forests, and Supply Chain programs. The scoring methodology assesses the level of detail and comprehensiveness of a company's response, as well as its awareness of environmental issues, management methods, and progress toward environmental stewardship. CDP's scoring partners produce scores based on the data provided in company responses and the methodology is available online for transparency. The scoring system is divided into four levels: Disclosure, Awareness, Management, and Leadership, with companies being assessed and awarded points at each level. The points are then converted into a percentage, providing a snapshot of how a company compares with others in their sector. The scoring system is mission-driven, focusing on CDP's principles and values for a sustainable economy, and aims to drive changes in company behavior to improve environmental performance.

FTSE Russell: FTSE Russell's ESG Ratings and data model provide investors with a comprehensive understanding of a company's exposure and management of ESG issues. The data is flexible and customizable and is built on over 300 individual indicator assessments that are applied to each company's unique circumstances. The ESG Scores are calculated using an Exposure-weighted average, meaning that the most material ESG issues are given the most weight when determining a company's scores. FTSE Russell's ESG data model is overseen by an independent external committee and supports alignment with the UN Sustainable Development Goals (SDGs). The data is designed to assist in managing exposure to ESG aspects, meet mandated stewardship requirements, integrate ESG data into securities and portfolio analysis, and implement ESG-aware investment strategies. The data collection process for FTSE Russell's ESG research relies on publicly disclosed information only and companies are allowed to provide feedback and additional information that could be factored into the analysis.

Refinitiv ESG Score: Refinitiv's ESG Score provide a transparent and objective measurement of a company's environmental, social, and governance performance, commitment, and effectiveness. Based on publicly available data, the scores are calculated, which are grouped into 10 categories that form the three pillar scores.

These categories include emissions, environmental product innovation, human rights, shareholders, and more. Refinitiv's ESG score reflects the underlying ESG data framework, considering industry materiality and company size biases. The final ESG score reflects the company's performance, commitment, and effectiveness based on publicly reported information. It allows investors to understand a company's exposure to ESG issues, helping them make informed investment decisions. Companies are given access to review and provide feedback on the data used in the assessment, and Refinitiv's team of analysts will determine if a change in assessment is warranted.

RepRisk: RepRisk is a leading provider of ESG research and ratings for private and public companies. Founded in 1998, the company offers reports for more than 84,000 companies in 34 sectors globally, as well as over 14,000 NGOs and 10,000 governmental bodies. RepRisk's rating scale ranges from AAA to D, with updates provided daily. The company's methodology involves screening relevant data from over 80,000 media and stakeholder sources, with a focus on 28 ESG issues that are divided into environmental, community relations, employee relations, and corporate governance categories. Additionally, RepRisk also examines 45 specific ESG hot topics. Companies are invited to participate in a formal data verification process before the publication of their ESG ratings reports. RepRisk has formed partnerships with organizations such as the Carbon Disclosure Project and the United Nations-supported Principles of Responsible Investment. RepRisk's company reports, and Director's Briefs can be accessed through the company's ESG Risk Platform or bought individually.

Thomson Reuters ESG Research Data : Thomson Reuters ESG Research Data provides a comprehensive analysis of environmental, social, and governance (ESG) factors for public companies.

The company uses a percentile rank scoring methodology to calculate its ESG scores, which are based on over 400 different ESG metrics that are grouped into 10 categories: Resource use, emissions, innovation, management, shareholders, CSR strategy, workforce, human rights, community, and product responsibility. Each category is weighted based on the number of measures it contains, with categories that have multiple issues, such as management, having a higher weight than lighter categories such as human rights. The company also includes an analysis of 23 "Controversy Topics" in its ESG Score, which covers topics such as business ethics, intellectual property, public health, and human rights. The ESG Scores are available on the Thomson Reuters Eikon platform, but it is not specified how the data is used by investors or if companies can provide input or feedback on their scores.

Dow Jones Sustainability Index (DJSI) : The Dow Jones Sustainability Index is a float adjusted market capitalization weighted index that measures the performance of companies selected based on Environmental, Social, and Governance (ESG) criteria using a best-in-class approach. The DJSI is created in partnership with S&P Global Sustainable, a specialist in ESG research and data, to provide investors with objective benchmarks for managing their sustainability investment portfolios. The DJSI index family includes sub-indices that exclude companies engaged in certain activities widely considered unsustainable. The DJSI benchmarks are comprised of three geographical breakdowns: DJSI World, DJSI Regions, and DJSI Countries. The key factor in selecting constituents for any DJSI index is a company's S&P Global ESG Score, calculated under the S&P Global Corporate Sustainability Assessment (CSA). Companies are assessed based on their industry classification on the last business day of March, and if a company changes its domicile or industry, it will be eligible under its new classification starting with the subsequent assessment cycle. In the case of multiple classes of stock, only the stock with the largest float-adjusted market capitalization is considered for selection.

EcoVadis_: The EcoVadis methodology aims to measure the quality of a company's sustainability management system through its policies, actions, and results. The assessment evaluates 21 sustainability criteria that are grouped into four themes: Environment, Labour & Human Rights, Ethics, and Sustainable Procurement. These criteria are based on international sustainability standards such as the UN Global Compact, the International Labour Organization (ILO) conventions, the Global Reporting Initiative (GRI) standards, the ISO 26000 standard, the CERES Roadmap, and the UN Guiding Principles on Business and Human Rights. EcoVadis provides web-based collaboration tools for businesses, which allow procurement executives to access easy-to-use, dynamic scorecards, and to monitor the sustainability performance of their trading partners as well as their continuous improvement actions. The EcoVadis process includes seven management principles, 21 CSR criteria across four themes, a data collection and rating process, a diversity of data sources, and technology and CSR expert analysis. To participate in the EcoVadis assessment, companies can register online and create a company profile, specifying their business activity, contact information, etc. They will then answer a customised questionnaire and upload supporting documents. The questionnaire is secure, confidential, and multilingual with a support team ready to help. Once completed, EcoVadis analysts will distil the answers into a Scorecard, an independent questionnaire, and a document-based management system assessment. Companies can access their

Scorecard results online, share them, collaborate with customers, improve their performance, and broadcast their success.

The Corporate Knights Global 100: The Corporate Knights Global 100 is an annual ranking of the world's most sustainable corporations, published in 2005. The ranking is conducted by Corporate Knights, a specialized media and investment research firm based in Toronto. Corporate Knights is an employee- owned B Corp that operates in three segments: Corporate Knights Magazine, Corporate Knights Research, and Council for Clean Capitalism. The Global 100 ranking is based on a rigorous assessment of public companies with revenue over $1 billion and is based mostly on publicly disclosed data. The ranking is based on up to 24 key performance indicators covering resource management, employee management, financial management, clean revenue & clean investment, and supplier performance. Eligibility for the ranking is based on size and Corporate Knights Industry Group and geography. The ranking is meant to be representative of business sustainability in the current socio- economic context and is transparent, objective, and based on public data. Companies are compared against their Corporate Knights Industry Group peers and stakeholders' feedback is actively solicited throughout the project.

(Source : www.iriscarbon.com)

Building upon the preceding discussion of ESG data models and methodology, it is vital to recognise that while independent oversight and alignment with global standards (such as the UN SDGs) help enhance credibility, the reliance on publicly disclosed information and company feedback introduces variability in data quality and completeness. This can lead to differences in how ESG factors are interpreted and scored across rating agencies, especially as each provider applies its own analytical approach and weighting systems. With this background It is significant to analyse the study by Billio, M et al., (2021), to understand the similarities , variances , source data , number of criteria , main risk factors etc. used by ESG rating agencies in arriving at the score.

Table 5: Key differences between major ESG rating agencies

	MSCI	Vigeo- Eiris	Refinitiv	Sustainalytics	ISS Oekom	RobecoSAM	ECPI	Bloomberg	FTSE Russell
Rating score	CCC to AAA	-- to ++	D- to A+ and 0 to 100	0 to 100	D- to A+	0 to 100	F to EEE	0 to 100	0 to 5
History	1990	1983	2002	1992	1985	1995	1997	2008	2001
Headquarter	New York, United States	Paris, France	Toronto, Canada	Amsterdam, Netherlands	Munich, Germany	Zurich, Switzerland	Milan, Italy	New York, United States	London, United Kingdom
Sources	Company disclosure, 1600+ Media sources, 100+ specialized dataset	Company disclosure, Recommendation, Conventions	Company websites, Company reports, NGO websites, Media and news, Stock exchange filings	Public disclosure, Media and news, NGO reports	Publicly available information, Interview with stakeholders, information on company policies and practices, company direct contact	Survey approach	Company reports, Media and news, Regulatory data, Bloomberg and Thomson Reuters, University networks	Company reports, Publicly available information, Company direct contact	Publicly available information, Company direct contact, Other sources (governments and NGOs)
N. Criteria	37	38	178	155	100	74	80/86	120	300
Main risk factors	*Environmental* Climate change, Natural resources, Pollution and waste, Management, Environmental opportunities *Social* Product liability, Human capital, Stakeholder needs, Social opportunities *Governance* Corporate behavior, Corporate governance	Human resources, Human rights, Environment, Business behavior, Community, Involvement, Corporate governance	*Environmental* Resource use, Emission, Innovation *Social* Workforce, Human rights, Community, Product responsibility *Governance* Management, Shareholders, CSR strategy	Industry-specific indicators. Factors change according to the industrial group to which a company belongs	*Environment* Climate change strategy, Ecoefficiency, Energy Mgmt, Env. impact of product, Env. Mgmt, water risk and impact *Social* Equal opportunities, Freedom of association, Health and safety, Human rights, Product responsibility, Social impact of product, Supply chain mgmt, Taxes *Governance* Business ethics, Compliance, Independence of the board, Remuneration, Shareholder democracy and structure	About 21 Industry-Specific indicators. Three main dimensions: *Economic* (38/100) *Environmental* (27/100) *Social* (35/100)	*Environmental* Environmental strategy policy, Environmental Mgmt, Products, Production process *Social & Governance* Employees and human capital, Community relations, Markets, Corporate governance & shareholder	*Environmental* Carbon emissions, Climate change effect, Pollution, Waste disposal, Renewable energy, Resource depletion *Social* Supply chain, Political contributions, Discrimination, Diversity, Community relations, Human rights, *Governance* Cumulative voting, Executive compensation, Shareholders' Rights, Takeover Defense, Staggered boards, Independent directors	*Environmental* Biodiversity, Climate change, Pollution & resources, Water security, Supply chain *Social* Labor standards, Human rights & community, Health & safety, Customer responsibility, Supply chain *Governance* Tax transparency, Risk management, Corporate governance, Anti-corruption

(Source: Billio, M., Costola, M., Hristova, I., Latino, C. and Pelizzon, L., 2021. Inside the ESG ratings:(Dis) agreement and performance.)

The chart presented by Billio, M. et al. (2021) provides valuable insights into the methodologies employed by ESG rating agencies. It facilitates a comprehensive understanding of the key similarities and differences in their approaches, including the source data utilised, the number of criteria assessed, and the principal risk factors considered when determining ESG scores. Such analysis is instrumental in appreciating why ESG ratings diverge so sharply.

CHAPTER 5
DATA, DISCLOSURE, AND DOUBLE MATERIALITY

WHY MORE DATA DOES NOT MEAN BETTER ALIGNMENT

The rapid expansion of ESG data was expected to resolve inconsistencies in sustainability assessment. Instead, it has intensified divergence. More disclosure, more indicators, and more analytical tools have not produced convergence among ESG ratings. This outcome appears counterintuitive until the dynamics of data, disclosure, and materiality are examined more closely.

Corporate ESG disclosure has grown exponentially over the past decade. Sustainability reports, integrated reports, climate disclosures, human capital statements, and supply chain audits now accompany traditional financial filings. Regulatory initiatives and voluntary frameworks have encouraged greater transparency, often with the assumption that improved data availability would naturally lead to better comparability. In practice, disclosure has increased volume far more than coherence.

One source of divergence lies in the heterogeneity of disclosures. Companies report ESG information using different frameworks, metrics, and scopes. Even when aligned to common standards, disclosures vary in depth, methodology, boundary definitions, and assurance quality. ESG rating agencies must therefore interpret, normalize, and supplement reported data, introducing judgment at multiple stages.

Data gaps further complicate assessment. Not all companies disclose the same information, and smaller firms or those operating in emerging markets often report less comprehensively. Rating agencies respond by estimating missing data using models, proxies, or peer averages. These estimation techniques differ significantly across providers, amplifying divergence rather than reducing it.

The rise of alternative data sources has added complexity. Media screening, NGO reports and social media analysis are increasingly used to capture real-time ESG signals. While these sources enrich analysis, they also introduce variability in signal interpretation, controversy scoring, and temporal weighting. Identical events may be classified differently across rating systems, producing inconsistent outcomes.

Materiality frameworks sit at the center of this complexity. Financial materiality focuses on sustainability factors that affect enterprise value, while double materiality extends assessment to impacts on society and the environment irrespective of financial relevance. Both perspectives are increasingly embedded in regulation and investor practice. However, ESG rating agencies operationalize materiality differently, selecting indicators and weights that reflect their chosen lens. Without calibration, these differing materiality perspectives cannot be reconciled. A company may perform well under a financially material lens while performing poorly under an impact-oriented assessment, or vice versa. Neither assessment is inherently wrong, but their coexistence without translation mechanisms confuses end users and undermines decision clarity.

Crucially, more data does not resolve this tension. In the absence of a common interpretive framework, additional indicators simply expand the space for divergence. ESG assessments become more detailed but less comparable. Transparency increases, yet intelligibility declines.

This chapter challenges the assumption that disclosure alone can fix ESG rating inconsistencies. Data is a necessary input, but it is not a solution. Without calibration, expanding disclosure regimes risk reinforcing the Calibration Paradox rather than resolving it. The following chapter examines the tangible costs of this divergence for markets, institutions, and sustainability outcomes.

The evaluation sheets, tailored for each industry, are assessed through a comprehensive system-level approach rather than by focusing exclusively on individual transactions. This method ensures that all relevant system-related queries specific to the industry are addressed. Moreover, the data and information utilized in this evaluation are sourced directly from the company itself, representing the most reliable source and ensuring that neither third-party nor external information is included in the assessment.

The weighting factors employed in the calculation are based on globally recognized indexes, thereby meeting the requirements for the three ESG elements—Environment, Social, and Governance. As these indexes are country-specific, appropriate weights are assigned according to the geographies in which the company operates. Additionally, business volume, which may fluctuate annually, is incorporated as a factor in the final formula for the Global ESG score. To address existing gaps, a new rating formula —**ESG QUANTA CALIBRATOR**—has been introduced.

CHAPTER 6
THE COST OF DIVERGENCE

For many people, the divergence in ESG ratings sounds like a technical issue. A methodological disagreement between analysts. A difference in scoring systems.

But the reality is far more consequential.

When ESG ratings diverge, the impact travels far beyond spreadsheets and scorecards. It reaches investors making billion-dollar decisions, companies shaping long-term strategy, regulators designing policy, and ultimately the public that expects sustainability to mean something real.

The cost of divergence is not abstract. It is systemic.

For investors, ESG ratings are supposed to act as a compass. They help identify risks, opportunities, and responsible companies. But when different rating agencies assign drastically different scores to the same company, the compass begins to spin.

Two asset managers may believe they are pursuing the same sustainability strategy. Yet if they rely on different ESG datasets, their portfolios can end up looking completely different. One may hold companies that another excludes. One may avoid risks the other unknowingly embraces.

What begins as a methodological difference soon becomes a problem of accountability. Investors must explain decisions to clients, pension funds, and regulators. When ESG scores themselves cannot agree, the credibility of ESG investing begins to weaken.

The problem becomes even more visible in passive investing.

Many ESG funds follow indices that rely on rating thresholds to decide which companies are included. But if those ratings differ from one provider to another, the resulting indices also diverge.

Two ESG funds may appear similar on the surface. Their names might suggest the same sustainability philosophy. Yet under the hood, their holdings could be fundamentally different. Investors who expect comparable outcomes may instead find themselves exposed to entirely different sustainability profiles.

Companies experience this confusion from the other side.

Corporate leaders increasingly invest time and resources into sustainability programs. They improve governance practices, reduce environmental footprints, and strengthen social initiatives. But when ESG ratings diverge, the feedback they receive from the market becomes inconsistent.

An initiative that improves a company's rating with one provider may barely move the needle with another. In some cases, it might even lower the score.

This creates a strange and frustrating reality for management teams. Instead of focusing purely on meaningful sustainability outcomes, they may find themselves managing perceptions across multiple rating systems. Reporting requirements multiply. Communication strategies become fragmented. Internal alignment becomes harder to maintain.

Gradually, attention shifts away from genuine progress toward the optimization of scores.

The financial consequences can also be very real.

Today, many loans and bonds are tied to ESG performance. Sustainability-linked financing instruments often adjust interest rates based on ESG metrics or ratings. If a company's ESG score changes, the cost of financing can change as well.

But when ratings diverge, these financial consequences can become unpredictable. A score might change not because the company's behaviour changed, but because the rating methodology was revised. Yet the impact on financing costs, investor perception, and corporate reputation can be immediate.

In such situations, companies may find themselves paying more for capital even though their underlying sustainability performance remains unchanged.

Regulators face an even broader challenge.

Around the world, policymakers are increasingly integrating ESG concepts into disclosure rules, taxonomies, and supervisory frameworks. Their goal is to create greater transparency and guide capital toward sustainable outcomes.

But if regulators indirectly rely on ESG ratings that are inconsistent or opaque, private methodological biases may quietly enter public policy. Two companies could receive very different regulatory scrutiny simply because of differences in rating frameworks.

The result is uneven treatment, distorted incentives, and a loss of confidence in the system itself.

Beyond investors, companies, and regulators lies an even larger consequence: public trust.

Sustainability is a collective endeavor. It relies on the belief that progress can be measured, compared, and improved over time. When ESG ratings send conflicting signals, that belief begins to erode.

Critics quickly point to these inconsistencies as evidence that ESG is subjective or unreliable. Supporters struggle to explain why one company can simultaneously be considered a leader by one agency and a laggard by another.

The conversation shifts away from solutions and toward skepticism.

In the long run, this confusion carries a deeper cost. Capital, effort, and attention begin to flow toward optimizing ratings rather than improving real-world outcomes. Companies that genuinely lead in sustainability may not always be recognized. Others may benefit from superficial improvements that align better with particular rating models.

The signal becomes buried in noise.

At a time when clarity is most needed, the system becomes harder to interpret.

This is why ESG divergence cannot be dismissed as a harmless byproduct of analytical diversity. Diversity of perspectives is valuable. But when that diversity produces persistent incoherence, the entire ecosystem begins to lose effectiveness.

What the system needs is not uniformity, but calibration.

A framework that can preserve analytical diversity while restoring coherence across measurements. A way to interpret ESG signals without eliminating the richness of different methodologies.

This is where the **ESG Quanta Calibrator Score** enters the conversation.

The ESG Quanta Calibrator provides investors with a clearer lens through which to evaluate companies. It highlights potential operational, regulatory, and reputational risks that may influence a company's long-term stability and its ability to continue as a going concern.

At the same time, it offers valuable insight to corporate decision-makers. By identifying vulnerabilities and inconsistencies, policy-makers within organizations can take corrective steps that reduce both present and future risks.

A strong ESG Quanta Calibrator score often reflects more than just compliance. It signals resilience, stronger brand value, higher customer satisfaction, and improved productivity.

At its core, ESG is about balance.

Environmental responsibility, social well-being, and sound governance are not competing priorities. In a healthy and civilized society, they carry equal weight. Businesses do not operate in isolation from the communities and ecosystems that sustain them.

They have a responsibility to contribute positively to both.

But responsibility alone is not enough. Progress must also be measured.

The principle is simple: if something cannot be measured, it cannot be evaluated. And if it cannot be evaluated, it cannot be improved.

Regular and thoughtful measurement allows organizations to track their progress, identify gaps, and strengthen their sustainability strategies over time. Companies that manage ESG issues effectively often discover that they are not sacrificing value. Instead, they are protecting and enhancing it.

By anticipating regulatory shifts, mitigating risks early, and exploring new opportunities in emerging markets, they create durable advantages.

They also build something less tangible but equally powerful: reputation.

A company's commitment to environmental stewardship, social responsibility, and ethical governance contributes to brand equity in ways that extend far beyond financial statements.

In the long run, investors benefit from this as well.

Successful investment ultimately depends on the health of the broader economy. And a healthy economy depends on a stable society and a sustainable planet.

Financial markets therefore have a clear self-interest in encouraging responsible environmental and social behavior. When ESG considerations are thoughtfully integrated into investment decisions, markets tend to become more stable and more predictable.

But ESG is not a short-term project.

Its impact unfolds over years and decades, not quarters. Expecting immediate results from ESG initiatives misunderstands their nature. Sustainability transformations require patience, consistency, and long-term commitment.

The rewards, however, are profound.

ESG has the potential to reshape how businesses operate, how investors allocate capital, and how societies pursue progress.

In the chapters that follow, we will explore the foundational principles required to build an ESG framework capable of delivering this impact. A framework that restores clarity, strengthens trust, and aligns sustainability measurement with the outcomes that truly matter.

PART THREE
THE ESG QUANTA CALIBRATOR

CHAPTER 7
FIRST PRINCIPLES OF CALIBRATION

If ESG rating divergence is a structural problem, its solution must also be structural. Calibration is not a cosmetic adjustment applied after scores are produced. It is a foundational design principle that determines whether diverse assessments can coexist meaningfully within a single decision environment.

In measurement science, calibration refers to the process of aligning different instruments to a shared reference so that their outputs can be compared, interpreted, and trusted. Financial markets rely on calibrated systems, common accounting standards, benchmark yield curves, and standardized risk measures. Diversity of analysis exists, but interpretation converges because reference frames are shared. ESG assessment lacks this condition.

The first principle of ESG calibration is reference coherence. ESG scores must be interpretable relative to a common baseline that is independent of any single rating methodology.

Without such a baseline, scores remain internally valid but externally incomparable. Calibration does not eliminate methodological differences; it translates them.

The second principle is plurality preservation. Sustainability is inherently multidimensional and context-specific. Any attempt to force uniformity risks erasing material nuance and legitimate analytical disagreement. Calibration must therefore operate at a meta-level, allowing multiple methodologies to coexist while enabling their outputs to be mapped onto a common interpretive space.

The third principle is materiality neutrality. ESG calibration cannot privilege a single definition of materiality. Financial materiality, impact materiality, and double materiality represent different lenses, not errors. A calibrated framework must accommodate these perspectives without collapsing them into a single score that obscures intent. Translation, not substitution, is required.

The fourth principle is sectoral and contextual sensitivity. ESG performance is not absolute. It is shaped by industry characteristics, geographic context, regulatory regimes, and transition pathways. Calibration must normalize scores without flattening these differences. Comparability must not come at the cost of relevance.

The fifth principle is transparency of transformation. Calibration processes must be intelligible to end users. While underlying methodologies may remain proprietary, the logic by which scores are translated into a common reference frame must be clear. Trust cannot be restored through opacity.

Finally, calibration must be decision oriented. The objective is not theoretical elegance but practical usability. Investors, corporates, and regulators require ESG assessments that support comparison, trend analysis, and forward-looking judgment. Calibration should reduce noise, not add complexity.

The need to develop the **ESG Quanta Calibrator** arises from significant disparities in ESG ratings assigned by different rating agencies to the same company. Detailed analysis reveals both major and minor variations in the assessment of the three ESG components—Environmental (E), Social (S), and Governance (G) —as well as in consolidated scores. The absence of a uniform global reporting standard for ESG leads to confusion and makes meaningful comparison challenging. As a result, the calibration process becomes essential to provide clarity and consistency for stakeholders seeking to interpret and compare ESG performance across diverse rating systems.

To achieve a global ESG score, it is essential that data be standardized to a consistent reporting period and currency across all countries of operation. The lack of a universally accepted ESG reporting standard complicates meaningful comparisons and increases confusion within the market. For the purposes of calculating business volume, a uniform currency is applied throughout the year, ensuring that financial data remains comparable across jurisdictions. This uniformity is critical for producing reliable ESG assessments that stakeholders can trust and utilize effectively in their decision-making processes.

These principles establish the conceptual foundation for a calibrated ESG ecosystem. They clarify what calibration is and, equally important, what it is not. The following chapter operationalizes these principles through the ESG Quanta Calibrator, translating theory into a functional framework.

CHAPTER 8
THE ESG QUANTA CALIBRATOR EXPLAINED

VARIABLES, LOGIC, AND NORMALIZATION FRAMEWORK

The ESG Quanta Calibrator is designed as a meta-framework that aligns disparate ESG ratings to a shared interpretive reference without replacing or overriding existing methodologies. Its purpose is not to produce yet another ESG score, but to enable coherence across scores.

At its core, the Quanta Calibrator treats each ESG rating as a signal rather than a verdict. Individual ratings contain valuable information, but that information is conditioned by methodology, materiality lens, data treatment, and weighting logic. Calibration extracts and normalizes these signals so that they can be meaningfully compared.

The framework operates through four sequential layers.

The first layer is signal normalization. ESG scores from different providers are rescaled to a common quantitative range using statistical normalization techniques that preserve relative positioning within each methodology. This step removes distortions arising from differing score distributions, scales, and rating bands.

The second layer is contextual anchoring. Normalized scores are adjusted for sectoral, geographic, and regulatory context. This anchoring ensures that performance is interpreted relative to relevant peer environments rather than against abstract global averages. Contextual anchoring prevents false equivalence between structurally different operating conditions.

The third layer is materiality translation. Rather than enforcing a single materiality lens, the Quanta Calibrator maps scores across financial, impact, and double materiality dimensions. This allows users to understand how a company performs under different sustainability perspectives and where divergences originate. Translation matrices make these relationships explicit rather than implicit.

The fourth layer is convergence analysis. Calibrated outputs are analyzed to identify zones of agreement, divergence, and uncertainty across rating methodologies. Instead of collapsing results into a single number, the framework produces a calibrated ESG profile that highlights robustness and fragility in assessment.

The output of the ESG Quanta Calibrator is therefore not a monolithic score, but a structured interpretive dashboard. Users can see where ESG assessments align, where they diverge, and why. Decision-makers gain clarity without sacrificing complexity.

Crucially, the Quanta Calibrator is methodology-agnostic. It does not require rating agencies to change their models or disclose proprietary formulas. By restoring a common reference frame, the ESG Quanta Calibrator resolves the Calibration Paradox without imposing standardization. It transforms ESG ratings from competing truths into calibrated perspectives.

The **ESG QUANTA CALIBRATOR** study commences by identifying gaps in the existing situation through a professional evaluation of the current rating mechanism. The primary purpose of the study is to derive a new formula by addressing the deficiencies present in the current evaluation process of the ESG Rating mechanism.

The three major steps in arriving at Score by **ESG QUANTA CALIBRATOR** are :

- Category score - for all the three elements of ESG (Industry specific)
- Country ESG Score
- Global ESG Score

ESG QUANTA CALIBRATOR address the existing gaps on criteria, system evaluation, data source and scoring; industry specific evaluation sheets are prepared for all the three elements of ESG viz Environment, Social and Governance, respectively. This focuses on system evaluation than transaction analysis. All the system check points related to the three elements, relevant to specific industry have been included in the evaluation sheet. This evaluation sheets are verified by a professional by checking the data from the company itself. So, the data source or the evaluation is done within the company. No third-party information, web site data, media source, NGO reports etc are considered. The entire evaluation is done based on the data and information available and shared by the company itself. This will enhance the cred-itability and reliability of the evaluation. All the three elements are given equal weightage. Every operating country will have a separate evaluation process for deriving category score. This will help in year-on-year comparison at country level, which is lacking in the existing scoring mechanism. To match the arithmetical equation, average percentage of each element of ESG is taken by the evaluator. So, the category score for each element of ESG will be done by a professional applying his experience and expertise.

The Environment, Social and Governance condition will vary from country to country. Even though the same company operates in different countries, the Environment, Social and Governance conditions will vary due to different geography. To arrive at ESG score for the country, a justifiable country specific weightage must be applied to each element of ESG. After a detailed and through evaluation, three country specific indexes have been identified. The main criteria for index selection, in addition to parameters are , that it should be published by a globally reputed organisation and there should be an index for every country.

The selected indexes are:

- Environment Performance Index (EPI)
- Social Progress Index (SPI)
- World Governance Index (WGI)

The parameters for Environment Performance Index are, climate mitigation, air quality, sanitation & drinking water, waste management, biodiversity, agriculture etc. It is published by Yale University and Columbia University in collaboration with the World Economic Forum. Environmental Performance Index (EPI) provides a data-driven summary of the state of sustainability around the world. It uses various performance indicators across 11 issue categories. EPI ranks about 180 countries on climate change performance, environmental health, and ecosystem vitality. These indicators provide a gauge at a country level scale to establish environmental policy targets. The EPI offers a scorecard that highlights leaders and laggards in environmental performance and provides practical guidance for countries that aspire to move toward a sustainable future. EPI indicators provide a way to spot problems, set targets, track trends, understand outcomes, and identify best policy practices, going beyond the aggregate scores and drilling down into the data to analyse performance by issue category, policy objective, peer group, and country offers even greater value for policymakers. This granular view and comparative perspective can assist in understanding the determinants of environmental progress and in refining policy choices.

(Source : https://epi.yale.edu)

Natural Capital Index was also considered for the weightage purpose. The natural capital index of a country is defined by the natural physical environment. The natural capital model incorporates the essence of resources that allow a country to be completely self-sustaining: land, water, climate, biodiversity, food production and capacity, and energy and mineral resources. In addition, the level of depletion or degradation of those resources that could endanger future self-sufficiency are considered to reflect the full picture of the available natural capital. The Natural Capital Index is based on 33 quantitative indicators, forming 6 clusters – water, other natural resources, biodiversity, food security, infrastructure and nature, and exposure to climate risks.

(Source: https://solability.com)

Since EPI found to be the best fit, the study chooses it as weightage index for environment.

The parameters for Social Progress Index are, Equity & Inclusiveness, Personal Safety, Nutrition and Basic Medical Care, Wellness (including health, shelter, water and sanitation), access to basic knowledge, access to Information and Communication, Personal Rights, Personal freedom and choice, Access to Advanced Education etc.. Social Progress Index (SPI) prepared by a renowned NGO; Social Progress Imperative, fulfils the criteria, so it's taken as the index for weightage.

The Social Progress Index offers a rich framework for measuring the multiple dimensions of social progress, benchmarking success, and catalysing greater human wellbeing. Social Progress Index ranks about 179 countries on social progress. It measures at least some aspects of social progress across which covers more than 99.97% of the world's population. SPI is used as a tool to assess strengths and weaknesses, spur constructive dialogue, catalyse change, and improve people's lives. Progress on social issues does not automatically accompany economic development. Rising income usually brings major improvements in areas such as access to clean water, sanitation, literacy, and basic education. But on average, personal security is no better in middle-income countries than low-income ones and is often worse. And, too many people, regardless of income, live without full rights and experience discrimination or even violence based on gender, religion, ethnicity, or sexual orientation. Traditional measures of national income, such as GDP per capita, fail to capture the overall progress of societies. The Social Progress Index rigorously measures country performance on many aspects of social and environmental performance which are relevant for countries at all levels of economic development. It enables an assessment of not just absolute country performance, but also relative performance compared to a country's economic peers. The Social Progress Index also allows to assess a country's success in turning economic progress into improved social outcomes. Overall, the Social Progress Index provides the first concrete framework for benchmarking and prioritizing an action agenda, advancing both social and economic performance. The index is structured around 12 components and 53 distinct indicators. The framework not only provides an aggregate country score and ranking but also allows benchmarking on specific areas of strength and weakness. Transparency of measurement based on a comprehensive framework allows change-makers to set strategic priorities, acting upon the most pressing issues in their societies.

(Source : https://www.socialprogress.org)

The study has considered Social Capital Index for weightage purpose. The Social Capital of a nation is the sum of social stability and the well-being (perceived or real) of the entire population. Social capital generates social cohesion and a certain level of consensus, which in turn delivers a stable environment for the economy and prevents natural resources from being over-exploited. In addition to local historical and cultural influences, the social consensus in a society is affected by several factors: health care systems and their universal availability / affordability (measuring physical health); income and asset equality, which are correlated to crime levels; demographic structure (to assess the future generational balance within a society); freedom of expression and freedom from fear; and the absence of violent conflicts. Only in these circumstances can the economy flourish, generate value, jobs and income for the population. The Social Capital Index is based on indicators related to the following clusters:

- Health
- Equality
- Crime
- Freedom
- Satisfaction

(Source : https://solability.com)

Another index considered for the weightage element of Social is Human Development Index. The Human Development Index (HDI) is a statistic developed and compiled by the United Nations since 1990, to measure various countries' levels of social and economic development. It is composed of four principal areas of interest: mean years of schooling, expected years of schooling, life expectancy at birth, and gross national income (GNI) per capita.

This index is a tool used to follow changes in development levels over time and compare the development levels of different countries. The HDI was created to emphasize that people and their capabilities should be the ultimate criteria for assessing the development of a country, not economic growth alone. It uses components such as average annual income and educational expectations to rank and compare countries. Social advocates have criticized the HDI for not representing a broad enough measure of the quality of life and economists for providing little additional useful information beyond simpler measures of the economic standard of living.

(Source : https://hdr.undp.org)

Since SPI found to be a better fit, the study chose it as weightage index for Social.

The parameters for Governance Index are Rule of Law, Human Rights / Participation, Sustainable development, Peace / Security, Human development etc... Almost all the above parameters are considered in preparing World Governance Index (WGI) by World Bank. The Worldwide Governance Indicators report on six broad dimensions of governance for over 200 countries and territories. The six composite WGI measures are useful as a tool for broad cross-country comparisons and for evaluating broad trends over time.

(Source : https://www.worldbank.org)

The study also considered Global Governance index for the weightage of Governance element of ESG. Governance is responsible for and designs the environment in which the country's natural, social and intellectual capital can flourish to generate new and sustain existing wealth. The Global Governance Index evaluates the performance of a country's regulatory framework and infrastructure environment to facilitate sustainable competitiveness, based on 33 quantitative indicators. The Governance Index does not assess the quality of regulatory frameworks itself – only the qualitative outcomes.

(Source : https://solability.com)

Since WGI found to be a better fit, the study chooses it as weightage index for Governance.

To have arithmetical uniformity, percentile of all the three indexes is considered. This will give equal importance for all the three elements of ESG. The average score of the product of category score in the evaluation sheet and the respective index will give the country ESG Score

To arrive at **ESG QUANTA CALIBRATOR** score, data should be of a uniform period and uniform currency for all the operating countries.

Evaluation Score (E) = Average (Environment Score card total)

Evaluation Score (S) = Average (Social Score card total)

Evaluation Score (G) = Average (Governance Score card total)

The next step is to apply the correct weightages to the evaluation score and to arrive at the country score. For this, country specific weightages have been identified for Environment, Social and Governance. For environment, Environment Performance Index (EPI) is the weightage applied and for social, Social Performance Index (SPI) is the weightage applied. World Governance Index (WGI) is the weightage applied for Governance element of ESG. So, the formula for country score is:

Country ESG Score = **Average (Evaluation Score (E) * EPI + Evaluation Score (S) * SPI + Evaluation Score (G) * WGI)**

The **ESG QUANTA CALIBRATOR** score of a company will be the cumulative product to country ESG score and business volume.

ESG QUANTA CALIBRATOR SCORE = (Country ESG Score * Country's Business volume)

$$\mathbf{GS = \sum (CSi * BVi)}$$

The above ESG QUANTA formula answers all the identified gaps in the existing ESG rating mechanism. The Global score will be out of 100 or can be treated as percentage.

The **ESG QUANTA** formula findings are:

- This formula is simple and easy to understand.
- Focuses on system than transactions.
- Covers all the geographies a company operates, irrespective of size.
- Evaluation done based on the data from the company itself. No third- party data used.
- Globally accepted indexes used for weightage.
- Year on Year country level comparison possible.

The chapters that follow apply this framework to real-world cases, demonstrating how calibration restores decision usefulness in practice.

CHAPTER 9
WEIGHTING, CONTEXT, AND SECTOR NEUTRALITY

RESOLVING BIAS WITHOUT ERASING MATERIALITY

One of the most persistent sources of ESG rating divergence lies in weighting. Decisions about how much importance to assign to environmental, social, and governance factors, and to individual indicators within each pillar, embed value judgments that shape outcomes more than raw data itself. Without calibration, these judgments remain opaque and non-comparable. Traditional ESG ratings apply fixed or semi-dynamic weights based on internal materiality assessments. While often justified by sector relevance or risk exposure, these weights vary widely across providers. A governance issue that dominates one rating may be marginal in another. Such discrepancies are rarely visible to end users, yet they determine final scores.

The ESG Quanta Calibrator approaches weighting differently. Rather than imposing a single weighting structure, it separates measurement from interpretation. Raw ESG signals are preserved, while weighting effects are made explicit through calibrated translation layers. This allows users to see how much of a score is driven by weighting choices rather than underlying performance.

Context plays a critical role in this process. Sector neutrality does not mean treating all industries identically. It means normalizing performance relative to sector-specific constraints, transition pathways, and risk profiles. The Quanta Calibrator applies contextual normalization to ensure that high-impact sectors are neither unfairly penalized nor artificially rewarded.

Geographic and regulatory contexts are similarly incorporated. Companies operating under different regulatory regimes face different disclosure obligations, enforcement standards, and transition timelines. Calibration adjusts for these structural differences without excusing poor performance. Contextual sensitivity enhances fairness while preserving accountability.

By disentangling weighting effects from performance signals, the Quanta Calibrator enables more nuanced interpretation. Decision-makers can assess ESG performance under multiple weighting scenarios, identify sensitivity to methodological assumptions, and make more informed judgments.

This chapter demonstrates that weighting need not be a hidden source of distortion. When made transparent and contextualized, it becomes a tool for insight rather than confusion.

The **ESG QUANTA CALIBRATOR** study has been structured to enable maximum possible data collection, facilitated by the study and evaluation with case study focusing on freight forwarding industry. Additionally, a thorough examination was conducted to identify appropriate weightages and indexes.

Briefly, to avoid bias in the **ESG QUANTA CALIBRATOR** formula , key assumptions such as equal weightage assigned to the three ESG elements (Environment, Social, and Governance) is applied. Practical challenges in achieving complete coverage across all operating countries, as well as issues regarding, accuracy, professionalism, dependency, etc are addressed by technological advancements , AI applications etc.

In applying a qualitative research method, a substantial collection of reliable and relevant documents was scrutinised and analysed professionally. Through this process, the study derived **ESG QUANTA CALIBRATOR** formula for ESG rating, in order to address and bridge the identified deficiencies in the current rating mechanism. With the formula established, further testing was undertaken utilising real data with special focus to freight forwarding industry. Specifically, data from a multinational corporation spanning three years was applied to the formula to determine the **ESG QUANTA CALIBRATOR** score for the company. Additionally, global indices for environment, social, and governance, respective to each country, were integrated into the formula calculation.

The absence of a globally uniform reporting standard for ESG complicates comparison and adds to the confusion. For business volume calculation, a uniform currency is applied throughout the year.

To summarize, all these data must be analysed by a professional evaluator to arrive at a logical conclusion for gauging the evaluation score across the three elements of ESG.

Index data are unrelated to the company itself; rather, they constitute a weightage mechanism relevant to the geographies in which the company operates. The selected index is the result of an extensive evaluation process to identify the best fit for the three elements of ESG.

Business volume data is crucial for calculating the **ESG QUANTA CALIBRATOR** score according to the new formula. Its significance lies in integrating all operating geographies as intrinsic components of the **ESG QUANTA CALIBRATOR** score, weighted by their contribution to the company's global sales. This approach ensures that each geography's business volume proportionally influences the global ESG score, thereby linking financial performance to ESG evaluation to a certain degree.

PART FOUR
VALIDATION AND CASE STUDIES

CHAPTER 10
SAME COMPANY, DIFFERENT SCORES

EMPIRICAL DIVERGENCE ACROSS RATING AGENCIES

The practical consequences of uncalibrated ESG ratings are most visible when examining individual companies assessed by multiple providers. Numerous empirical studies have shown that correlations between ESG ratings for the same firm are often weak, particularly across environmental and social dimensions.

These discrepancies can be traced to methodological differences rather than performance volatility. Variations in indicator selection, controversy treatment, sector benchmarking, and weighting drive divergence. The company's underlying sustainability practices remain relatively stable, yet its ESG identity shifts depending on the rating lens applied.

For investors, such divergence complicates interpretation. Is the company genuinely improving or deteriorating, or has the methodology changed? For corporates, the lack of a coherent signal undermines strategic clarity. For regulators, it raises concerns about reliance on any single rating source.

This chapter establishes the empirical reality that ESG divergence is not theoretical. It manifests concretely at the firm level, affecting real decisions and outcomes. The following chapter applies the ESG Quanta Calibrator to this same case, demonstrating how calibration restores coherence.

Below table is the comparison of ESG score for four different companies by four different ESG rating agencies

Table 6: Comparison of ESG score of four companies by 4 different ESG rating agencies

Company	Sustainalytics	RobecoSAM	Refinitiv	MSCI
Nissan Motor Co., Ltd	6	77	72	CCC
Verizon Communications Inc.	91	20	67	BB
Oracle Corp. Jpn	78	8	63	BB
Goodman Group	86	21	58	AA

(Source : Billio, M., Costola, M., Hristova, I., Latino, C. and Pelizzon, L., 2021. Inside the ESG ratings:(Dis) agreement and performance.)

The evaluation of Environmental, Social, and Governance (ESG) ratings is subject to considerable variability, arising from differences in methodology, source data, criteria, and applied weightages. The lack of consideration given to operating geography, and the predominant focus on transaction-level analysis rather than comprehensive system evaluation, further exacerbate issues of data quality and reliability. These inconsistencies are compounded by the frequent non-disclosure of complete procedures and the volume of data analysed, which undermines transparency and makes it difficult to assess the robustness of the ratings provided. It is crucial that the volume of data reviewed aligns with the scale of the company and the breadth of its geographic operations.

Researches by Gibson Brandon et al., (2021), opines that, a lot of attention has been drawn to divergence of ratings issued by different ESG rating providers for the same firm. For example, in a Wall Street Journal article, Mackintosh (2018) points out that Tesla was rated highly by MSCI regarding environmental issues in 2018. In contrast, FTSE came to the opposite conclusion, rating Tesla poorly on environmental matters.

The study further states that rating disagreement is generally more pronounced for firms that belong to the consumer durables and telecommunications industries, providing important insights for financial analysts that cover firms from these sectors.

CHAPTER 11
APPLYING THE QUANTA CALIBRATOR

RECALIBRATED OUTCOMES AND CONVERGENCE ANALYSIS

Applying the ESG Quanta Calibrator to the case examined in the previous chapter reveals the power of calibration. When ESG scores from multiple providers are normalized, contextually anchored, and translated across materiality lenses, patterns of convergence emerge.

Areas of genuine agreement become visible. In the examined case, governance practices show strong alignment across rating systems once weighting distortions are removed. Environmental performance displays moderate convergence when sectoral context is applied. Social indicators reveal the greatest divergence, reflecting differing interpretations of labor and supply chain impacts.

Rather than producing a single reconciled score, the calibrated output presents a structured profile highlighting consensus, divergence, and uncertainty. Investors gain insight into which ESG dimensions are robust across methodologies and which require deeper due diligence. Corporates can identify where strategic improvements are likely to yield broad recognition rather than methodology-specific gains.

Importantly, calibration also improves trend analysis. Changes in calibrated scores more accurately reflect underlying performance shifts rather than methodological revisions. This enhances the credibility of ESG performance tracking over time.

This chapter demonstrates that calibration does not eliminate complexity. It organizes it. By restoring a common reference frame, the ESG Quanta Calibrator transforms ESG ratings from competing narratives into complementary perspectives. The final chapters examine the implications of this transformation for investors, corporates, and regulators.

In this chapter, a representative multinational Freight Forwarding company is examined with **ESG QUANTA CALIBRATOR**.

The three years data of an MNC, operating in 101 countries is taken for case study to apply **ESG QUANTA CALIBRATOR** formula. A general guideline is applied, that the sample should cover a business volume not less than 75 % and at least one country from every continent. The below list of countries has been selected and evaluation sheet for Environment, Social and Governance has been shared. The guidelines for evaluation are shared with the sheet. The percentage of business volume of the selected countries for 2020, 2021 & 2022 are 76.35 %, 78.13 % and 77.43 % respectively. Also, representation from all continents is ensured for sample selection. For business volume calculation uniform currency is applied throughout the year. To have a better clarity, the year-end figures are not converted to have uniformity.

Conversions happened as and when the transactions have taken place throughout the 100 + countries. Monthly exchange rates are applied.

Below is the list of countries selected for evaluation:

No	Country	Continent
1	USA	North America
2	Germany	Europe
3	China	Asia
4	Great Britain	Europe
5	France	Europe
6	Canada	North America
7	Netherlands	Europe
8	Belgium	Europe
9	Switzerland	Europe
10	Italy	Europe
11	Mexico	North America
12	Austria	Europe
13	Australia	Australia
14	South Africa	Africa
15	Brazil	South America

Evaluation sheets for Environment, Social and Governance are prepared for Freight Forwarding Industry. Evaluation sheets for Freight Forwarding industry are given in Appendix A, B & C for Environment, Social and Governance respectively. Evaluation sheet will change from Industry to Industry. Ample time has been given to each operating country/ entity to submit the full evaluation data. Being a case study, the respective departments were asked to evaluate their respective areas. Generally, Human resource department, Quality department, Operations department, Warehouse department, Compliance department, Finance department etc. are involved in getting the evaluation sheet fully evaluated. Out of the fifteen countries, eleven countries submitted the fully completed evaluation sheet before the cut off time. Four countries were not able to submit the fully completed evaluation sheet before the cut off time. The case study is done with the available data of the fully completed evaluation sheets. Since there is a change, the business volume, percentile must be recalculated for arriving at the case study ESG Score. This change need not be applied for a scenario, where data from 100 % of the operating counties are available.

Below is the status chart of data evaluation sample send & received fully:

No	Country	Continent	Status
1	USA	North America	Full data not received before cut off time
2	Germany	Europe	Full data received before cut off time
3	China	Asia	Full data received before cut off time
4	Great Britain	Europe	Full data received before cut off time
5	France	Europe	Full data received before cut off time
6	Canada	North America	Full data not received before cut off time
7	Netherlands	Europe	Full data received before cut off time
8	Belgium	Europe	Full data not received before cut off time
9	Switzerland	Europe	Full data received before cut off time
10	Italy	Europe	Full data received before cut off time
11	Mexico	North America	Full data not received before cut off time
12	Austria	Europe	Full data received before cut off time
13	Australia	Australia	Full data received before cut off time
14	South Africa	Africa	Full data received before cut off time
15	Brazil	South America	Full data received before cut off time

Due to some unavoidable reasons, full data from USA, Mexico, Canada, and Belgium were not received before cut-off time. So, the study must reclassify the business volume percentile. Also, representation from North America will be missing.

The data received from the fully completed evaluation sheets are analysed and collated for each element of ESG, viz. Environment, Social & Governance. All the numerical data are keyed into Excel file, where different Pivot tables are prepared to generate different reports, analysis sheets etc. Pivot tables are prepared for each element of ESG separately for three years.

The country wise score of evaluation sheet with respect to Environment is as below:

		Evaluation Score - Environment		
No.	Country	2020	2021	2022
1	Australia	90.79	90.79	77.15
2	Austria	96.48	96.48	85.37
3	Brazil	62.06	62.06	55.97
4	China	45.21	45.21	36.46
5	France	96.97	96.97	80.23
6	Germany	93.58	93.58	80.10
7	Great Britain	98.55	98.55	99.74
8	Italy	86.06	86.06	74.07
9	Netherlands	91.27	91.27	80.36
10	South Africa	52.24	52.24	47.75
11	Switzerland	98.79	98.79	84.60

After generating the evaluation report for environment, next Pivot table is prepared to generate evaluation report for Social.

The country wise score of evaluation sheet with respect to Social is as below:

		Evaluation Score - Social		
No	**Country**	**2020**	**2021**	**2022**
1	Australia	97.08	97.46	96.79
2	Austria	96.87	96.56	97.04
3	Brazil	78.56	77.79	78.53
4	China	70.51	70.65	72.45
5	France	95.09	95.25	94.85
6	Germany	97.96	97.51	97.77
7	Great Britain	94.99	95.27	94.92
8	Italy	93.62	93.45	93.93
9	Netherlands	98.26	97.78	98.05
10	South Africa	75.15	74.67	77.09
11	Switzerland	98.89	99.08	99.47

After generating the evaluation report for Social, next Pivot table is prepared to generate evaluation report for Governance.

The country wise score of evaluation sheet with respect to Governance is as below:

		Evaluation Score - Governance		
No.	Country	2020	2021	2022
1	Australia	92.95	94.58	95.42
2	Austria	93.12	92.85	90.06
3	Brazil	43.42	42.18	41.28
4	China	43.46	44.61	42.71
5	France	81.90	84.48	82.95
6	Germany	90.44	92.29	91.45
7	Great Britain	88.00	88.18	88.42
8	Italy	67.83	70.07	69.69
9	Netherlands	95.00	96.56	94.95
10	South Africa	53.68	51.61	48.25
11	Switzerland	98.63	99.58	100.00

The weightages are selected from globally accepted indexes, where the parameters for environment, social and governances meet. To have arithmetical uniformity, percentile score of each country has been arrived at and keyed into the excel file, where Pivot tables are prepared based on the keyed in data for report preparation and analysis.

Environment Index for the country is the percentile of Environment Performance Index of the respective year. The Environment Performance Index is published once in two years, so the index for 2021 will be the same as 2020. The Environment Performance Index for the years 2020, 2021 & 2022 for all the countries along with the percentile has been applied.

Below is the list of Environment Score (Percentile) for the countries in the case study:

	Environment Performance Index (Year Wise)		
Country	**2020**	**2021**	**2022**
Australia	90.79	90.79	77.15
Austria	96.48	96.48	85.37
Brazil	62.06	62.06	55.97
China	45.21	45.21	36.46
France	96.97	96.97	80.23
Germany	93.58	93.58	80.10
Great Britain	98.55	98.55	99.74
Italy	86.06	86.06	74.07
Netherlands	91.27	91.27	80.36
South Africa	52.24	52.24	47.75
Switzerland	98.79	98.79	84.60

Since EPI is published once in two years, the index for 2020 and 2021 will be the same.

Similarly, the next step is to collate the results of social element of ESG in the evaluation sheets. Pivot tables are prepared for three years. Social Index for the country is the percentile of Social Progress Index of the respective year. The Social Progress Index for the years 2020, 2021 & 2022 for all the countries along with the percentile has been applied.

Below is the list of Social Progress Index (Percentile) for the countries in the case study:

	Social Progress Index (Year Wise)		
Country	**2020**	**2021**	**2022**
Australia	97.08	97.46	96.79
Austria	96.87	96.56	97.04
Brazil	78.56	77.79	78.53
China	70.51	70.65	72.45
France	95.09	95.25	94.85
Germany	97.96	97.51	97.77
Great Britain	94.99	95.27	94.92
Italy	93.62	93.45	93.93
Netherlands	98.26	97.78	98.05
South Africa	75.15	74.67	77.09
Switzerland	98.89	99.08	99.47

Similarly, the next step is to collate the results of Governance element of ESG in the evaluation sheets. Pivot tables are prepared for three years. Governance Index for the country is the percentile of World Governance Index of the respective year. The World Governance Index for the years 2020, 2021 & 2022 for all the countries along with percentile has been applied.

Below is the list of World Governance Index (Percentile) for the countries in the case study:

	World Governance Index (Year Wise)		
Country	**2020**	**2021**	**2022**
Australia	92.95	94.58	95.42
Austria	93.12	92.85	90.06
Brazil	43.42	42.18	41.28
China	43.46	44.61	42.71
France	81.90	84.48	82.95
Germany	90.44	92.29	91.45
Great Britain	88.00	88.18	88.42
Italy	67.83	70.07	69.69
Netherlands	95.00	96.56	94.95
South Africa	53.68	51.61	48.25
Switzerland	98.63	99.58	100.00

After preparing the weightage indexes for environment, social and governance the next step is the grouping of evaluation sheet. Evaluation sheets for environment, social and governance have been grouped for three years.

Below is the three-year grouping of Indexed Environment Score:

	Environment Score		
Country	2020	2021	2022
Australia	65.07	76.42	66.60
Austria	71.40	74.29	66.59
Brazil	33.62	40.13	37.60
China	28.63	32.02	28.87
France	36.36	42.42	37.11
Germany	59.89	63.63	57.67
Great Britain	60.12	68.00	71.81
Italy	62.48	65.28	60.44
Netherlands	41.98	49.29	49.82
South Africa	34.48	35.52	32.47
Switzerland	68.33	71.62	64.15

On analysing the country wise environment score, Australia's score has increased in 2021 because of higher score in the evaluation sheet. But in 2022 it got reduced despite higher evaluation score. This is because the EPI percentile has reduced from 90.79 to 77.15. Similar is the case with Austria, Brazil, China, France Germany, Italy, South Africa, and Switzerland. Whereas, Environment score of Great Britain has increased in 2022, due to the combined effect of higher evaluation score and increase in index ranking.

Below is the three-year grouping of Indexed Social Score:

	Social Score		
Country	2020	2021	2022
Australia	81.55	81.87	96.79
Austria	54.25	54.07	93.16
Brazil	62.06	61.45	63.61
China	45.83	47.34	49.56
France	35.66	40.48	47.43
Germany	62.86	65.01	67.63
Great Britain	81.69	83.84	85.43
Italy	78.64	84.11	92.05
Netherlands	70.75	70.40	76.48
South Africa	61.38	60.98	62.96
Switzerland	56.04	56.15	60.51

There is no major variation in the percentile of social performance index for 2020, 2021 & 2022. The positive and negative variations are meagre. But the Social score for all the countries is showing positive trends. This is due to the continuing improvement which reflected in the evaluation sheet. Austria and Italy did well in 2022 compared to previous years. The lower score of China is due to low SPI percentile. But the low scores of France and Switzerland need to be further investigated. The primary observation is that the evaluator would have taken a very conservative view in his judgement. This is one of the limitations of this method. This can be overcome by rotation of evaluators. When it comes to real time rating, professional evaluators will be doing it. So, the chances of error can be reduced or minimised.

Below is the three-year grouping of Indexed Governance Score:

	Governance Score		
Country	2020	2021	2022
Australia	92.95	94.58	95.42
Austria	91.56	91.30	90.06
Brazil	43.42	42.18	41.28
China	43.46	44.61	42.71
France	81.90	84.48	82.95
Germany	90.44	92.29	91.45
Great Britain	86.53	86.71	86.94
Italy	67.83	70.07	69.69
Netherlands	79.96	87.71	86.24
South Africa	53.68	51.61	48.25
Switzerland	83.02	85.47	87.50

Governance, generally based on various policies framed by the company, viz. Privacy policy, Code of Conduct, Anti bribery policy, Information / Cyber security policy, confidential reporting, whistle blower policy etc. For an MNC operating in various countries, the policies are same and mostly monitored centrally. A good number of MNCs will have a centrally located confidential reporting, where anybody can report anonymously. So, the evaluation score will be almost uniform. Governance Score for a well-disciplined company will be higher than Environment and Social score, because of the simple reason that the company will have a professional approach to all the policy with respect to creation, modification and periodic review. The variance in governance score will be mainly due to difference in index, viz. World Governance Index. Low scores of China, Brazil and South Africa are due to comparatively lower index.

The next step of the case study is to arrive at country score, which is the average score of indexed environment, social and governance scores.

Below is the three-year score for the respective country:

	Country Score		
Country	2020	2021	2022
Australia	79.86	84.29	86.27
Austria	72.40	73.22	83.27
Brazil	46.37	47.92	47.49
China	39.31	41.32	40.38
France	51.31	55.80	55.83
Germany	71.06	73.64	72.25
Great Britain	76.11	79.51	81.39
Italy	69.65	73.15	74.06
Netherlands	64.23	69.13	70.85
South Africa	49.84	49.37	47.89
Switzerland	69.13	71.08	70.72

Brazil, China, and South Africa scored less than 50 in Country Score. This is not because the company in the respective country is not doing well with respect to ESG, but due to the comparatively lower EPI, SPI and WGI of the respective country. The general trend of year-on-year increase in score is a positive sign and an indication that the company is doing good with respect to ESG initiatives.

Below is the business volume data for three years, which is the percentile of business volume of the countries from which full data received before cut off time:

	Business Volume Percentile (Year wise)		
Country	**2020**	**2021**	**2022**
Australia	2.40	2.28	2.87
Austria	3.32	2.91	3.26
Brazil	2.38	2.64	2.83
China	9.93	20.85	20.52
France	13.22	10.84	9.42
Germany	36.81	34.77	34.62
Great Britain	15.35	11.43	10.74
Italy	3.75	3.46	3.59
Netherlands	6.07	5.23	5.26
South Africa	3.99	3.12	2.84
Switzerland	2.78	2.47	4.05
Total	**100.00**	**100.00**	**100.00**

Business volume figures have to be regrouped, since full details from four countries were not received before the cut off time. Data from USA, Canada, Mexico and Belgium are missing. So, representative sample from North America is missing. All the four countries are high index countries, and the final score will be comparatively less, if the data from these countries has been included. This will get offset, since we didn't take samples from low business volume countries, which have comparatively lesser indices.

The last stage is arriving at the final ESG Score for the company. This is the cumulative score of the product of country score and business volume.

Global ESG Score Calculation

	Country Score			Turnover Percentile			Global Score		
Country	2020	2021	2022	2020	2021	2022	2020	2021	2022
Australia	79.86	84.29	86.27	2.40	2.28	2.87	1.92	1.92	2.48
Austria	72.40	73.22	83.27	3.32	2.91	3.26	2.40	2.13	2.71
Brazil	46.37	47.92	47.49	2.38	2.64	2.83	1.10	1.27	1.34
China	39.31	41.32	40.38	9.93	20.85	20.52	3.90	8.62	8.29
France	51.31	55.80	55.83	13.22	10.84	9.42	6.78	6.05	5.26
Germany	71.06	73.64	72.25	36.81	34.77	34.62	26.16	25.61	25.01
Great Britain	76.11	79.51	81.39	15.35	11.43	10.74	11.68	9.09	8.74
Italy	69.65	73.15	74.06	3.75	3.46	3.59	2.61	2.53	2.66
Netherlands	64.23	69.13	70.85	6.07	5.23	5.26	3.90	3.62	3.73
South Africa	49.84	49.37	47.89	3.99	3.12	2.84	1.99	1.54	1.36
Switzerland	69.13	71.08	70.72	2.78	2.47	4.05	1.92	1.76	2.86
Total							**64.37**	**64.12**	**64.44**

The company's ESG score remains almost the same throughout three years close to 64 out of 100, which is good. On an in-depth analysis, the major observation is that, the business volume from China has doubled from almost 10 % to 20 %, which is a substantial business volume. The index of China is less compared to other countries. Considering this major observation, we can infer that the company is doing well in ESG despite the increase in business volume from low index countries, and also, marginal reduction in business volume from high index countries.

PART FIVE
IMPLICATIONS AND THE ROAD AHEAD

CHAPTER 12
WHAT THIS MEANS FOR INVESTORS

DECISION CLARITY AND RISK REALISM

For investors, ESG calibration represents a shift from score consumption to signal interpretation. In an uncalibrated environment, ESG integration is often reduced to selecting a preferred data provider and accepting its methodological assumptions as given. Calibration changes this dynamic by restoring agency to the investor.

Calibrated ESG assessments allow investors to distinguish between robust sustainability signals and methodology- driven noise. Areas of convergence across rating systems indicate dimensions of ESG performance that are resilient to analytical variation. Conversely, persistent divergence highlights domains that require deeper due diligence, engagement, or risk pricing.

Portfolio construction benefits directly from this clarity. Investors can build strategies that reflect intentional sustainability objectives while understanding the sensitivity of outcomes to materiality lenses and weighting assumptions. Calibration supports scenario analysis, enabling investors to assess how portfolios perform under different sustainability interpretations without constantly switching data providers.

Risk management is similarly strengthened. Calibrated ESG profiles improve the identification of transition risks, governance vulnerabilities, and social exposure by filtering out distortions caused by inconsistent scoring practices. This enhances forward-looking assessment and aligns ESG integration more closely with fiduciary responsibility.

Stewardship and engagement also gain precision. Investors can engage with companies on ESG issues that demonstrate cross-methodology relevance rather than pursuing narrowly defined rating improvements. This shifts dialogue from score optimization to substantive performance improvement.

Ultimately, calibration allows investors to treat ESG as decision intelligence rather than a compliance overlay. It supports disciplined capital allocation while preserving analytical diversity. As ESG continues to shape financial markets, calibrated interpretation will become a prerequisite for credible investment practice.

Calibrated ESG scores serve as a powerful tool for investors seeking to navigate complex financial landscapes with greater confidence. By providing a standardised measure of environmental, social, and governance factors, these scores enable more accurate comparisons between companies within the same sector. This not only streamlines the investment process but also ensures that decisions are based on reliable and consistent data, mitigating the risk of subjective or fragmented analysis.

Moreover, the ability to compare ESG scores across different industries broadens the horizon for investors. It allows for the identification of industries that are leading in sustainability practices as well as those lagging behind. In turn, this supports more informed portfolio diversification and risk management, as investors can assess potential opportunities and threats from a wider, more holistic perspective.

Another key advantage of using calibrated ESG scores lies in their capacity to inform timing decisions, such as when to enter or exit an investment. By tracking shifts in a company's or industry's ESG performance over time, investors can anticipate potential changes in reputation, regulatory standing, or operational resilience. This forward-looking insight helps to pinpoint optimal moments for increasing exposure to a promising sector or withdrawing from one that shows signs of decline.

Finally, for those considering additional investments in a specific company or industry, a calibrated ESG score offers a valuable reference point. It provides clarity on whether a target is improving or deteriorating in its ESG commitments, thus helping to align investment strategies with both financial objectives and ethical considerations. In an era where sustainability is increasingly linked to long-term value creation, leveraging calibrated ESG metrics has become an essential component of prudent investment decision-making.

CHAPTER 13
WHAT THIS MEANS FOR CORPORATES

STRATEGY, DISCLOSURE, AND LONG-TERM VALUE

For corporates, the proliferation of ESG ratings has often produced confusion rather than clarity. Companies face overlapping questionnaires, inconsistent evaluations, and conflicting signals about what constitutes good performance. Calibration offers a pathway out of this fragmentation.

A calibrated ESG framework enables companies to understand how their sustainability performance is interpreted across different rating methodologies. By revealing where assessments converge and diverge, calibration helps management distinguish between fundamental performance gaps and methodological artefacts.

Strategic prioritization improves as a result. Rather than allocating resources to optimize individual scores, companies can focus on initiatives that demonstrate cross-framework relevance and long-term impact. This strengthens the internal business case for sustainability investments and reduces strategic fatigue.

Disclosure strategy also benefits. Calibration clarifies which disclosures enhance interpretability across methodologies and which primarily serve specific rating models. Companies can streamline reporting, reduce redundancy, and improve narrative coherence without sacrificing transparency.

Governance implications are equally significant. Boards and executive teams gain clearer oversight of ESG performance, risk exposure, and strategic alignment. ESG metrics integrated into incentive structures become more credible when grounded in calibrated signals rather than isolated scores.

In a calibrated ecosystem, corporates are evaluated less on their ability to navigate rating complexity and more on the substance of their sustainability performance. This realignment supports long-term value creation and restores confidence in ESG as a strategic management tool.

A robust and well-calibrated ESG (Environmental, Social, and Governance) score is increasingly becoming a vital tool for corporates seeking to evaluate and enhance their sustainability efforts. By offering a comprehensive snapshot of a company's performance across key non-financial dimensions, this score enables organisations to pinpoint areas requiring improvement and benchmark themselves against industry peers. This process not only encourages healthy competition but also fosters a culture of continuous development within the business.

Furthermore, the transparency and clarity provided by a calibrated ESG score can strengthen a company's reputation among investors, employees, and business partners. Stakeholders are better equipped to assess the company's long-term value creation and sustainability, which contributes to increased confidence and can ultimately drive shareholder wealth. In today's market, where responsible investing is on the rise, such metrics play a critical role in attracting ethical investors and growth-oriented partners alike.

Additionally, leveraging ESG scores for strategic decision making empowers corporates to proactively address potential risks and capitalise on emerging opportunities. By understanding which components of ESG need enhancement, companies can implement targeted initiatives that not only align with regulatory expectations but also resonate with societal values. In turn, this holistic approach to value creation supports long-term business resilience and positions the organisation as a credible leader within its sector.

A distinct advantage of utilising calibrated ESG scores is the capacity to identify credible and growth-oriented business partners. By assessing ESG performance, organisations can select partners who demonstrate genuine commitment to responsible and sustainable practices. This, in turn, builds trust and lays the foundation for mutually beneficial collaborations, reduce potential risks , driving both business expansion and shared value creation.

CHAPTER 14
WHAT THIS MEANS FOR REGULATORS

TOWARDS GLOBAL ESG INTEROPERABILITY

Regulators face a growing challenge as ESG considerations become embedded in disclosure regimes, supervisory frameworks, and sustainable finance policies. While ESG ratings provide valuable inputs, their uncalibrated use risks introducing inconsistency and private methodological bias into public governance.

Calibration offers regulators a principled alternative. Rather than endorsing or standardizing specific ESG rating providers, regulators can require calibrated interpretive frameworks that translate diverse assessments into coherent signals. This preserves market innovation while enhancing regulatory reliability.

Policy design benefits from improved comparability. Calibrated ESG profiles support more consistent taxonomy alignment, supervisory assessment, and cross-border cooperation. They reduce the risk that regulatory outcomes depend on the choice of data vendor rather than underlying sustainability performance.

Calibration also supports proportional regulation. By highlighting areas of convergence and uncertainty, regulators can target supervisory attention where risks are most robustly identified, avoiding over-reliance on contested metrics. This improves regulatory efficiency and credibility.

At a systemic level, calibration strengthens the integrity of sustainable finance ecosystems. It aligns private ESG assessment with public policy objectives without collapsing diversity into uniformity. As sustainability challenges intensify, regulators will require tools that support coordination, comparability, and trust.

This chapter underscores that calibration is not merely a technical enhancement. It is an enabling infrastructure for credible ESG governance. With calibrated interpretation, ESG can evolve from fragmented assessment to coherent policy instrument.

A calibrated ESG score is an essential tool for regulators as they work to ensure compliance with legal frameworks and societal commitments. By providing a transparent and robust measurement of an organisation's sustainability performance, ESG scores give regulators the means to assess alignment with statutory obligations and ethical standards.

One of the key benefits of a calibrated ESG score is its value for benchmarking. Regulators can use ESG scores to compare organisations within and across industries, identifying those that set the standard for responsible business practices and highlighting areas where others may be falling short. This benchmarking process not only drives healthy competition but also encourages continual improvement among companies striving to enhance their ESG credentials. By establishing clear benchmarks, regulators can more effectively monitor trends, enforce compliance, and recognise leaders in sustainability.

The process of calibrating ESG scores involves aligning assessment criteria with both local and international standards. This ensures that compliance is not just a matter of ticking boxes but is genuinely embedded in organisational culture and operations. As a result, companies are motivated to go beyond the minimum legal requirements, adopting best practices that benefit both business and society.

Furthermore, having access to accurate and standardised ESG data streamlines regulatory oversight and fosters trust among a broad range of stakeholders. Transparent scoring mechanisms reassure investors, customers, and communities that organisations are genuinely committed to sustainable operations. In the long run, effective benchmarking and reliable ESG scores contribute to bolstering reputations, attracting investment, and supporting sustainable value creation for all involved.

From fragmented scores to calibrated truth - **ESG Quanta Calibrator.**

APPENDIX A

Category score card template for Freight Forwarding Industry:

No.	Item Head	Percentage	Guidelines
	Evaluation Score - Environment (Year)		
1	Environmental Policy	XX	Does the company have a written environment policy (including waste management) commensurate with its size of operation. How efficient is the policy implementation viz violation (if any) and corrective actions dealt with. Does the policy have periodic revision with respect to statutory requirement and technological upgradation.
2	Dangerous Goods Policy	XX	Does the company have a written DG matching with the requirements of freight forwarding industry. How efficient is the policy implementation viz violation (if any) and corrective actions dealt with. Does the policy have periodic revision with respect to statutory requirement and technological upgradation.
3	CO_2 Reduction - (Carbon neutral / GHG reduction etc)	XX	Does the company calculates emission trend (reduction over past 3 years) Does the company have initiated steps for net zero (GHG reduction projects), carbon neutral etc Does the company uses services of aircrafts flying with SAF, if yes % of total usage Does the company uses services of ships installed with scrubbers for removing sulphur from their exhaust, if yes % of total usage Does the company uses electric vehicles for road movement, if yes % of total usage.
4	Energy usage and efficiency	XX	Does the company took steps to improve efficiency in energy usage in heating, Cooling, Lighting, Power Source, LED, VRF (Variable Refringent flow) A/c, Inverter, UPS etc Does the company's warehouses and offices uses clean energy (Solar, Wind power etc) Whether the company have future plans to shift to 100 % renewable energy in office and WHs
5	Biodiversity	XX	Whether the company has initiated programs to educate the stake holders (employees, vendors, customers, public etc) on protection of planet, climate change, reduction of GHG, air & water preservation / pollution, bio diversity , reforestation , removal of plastic from ocean / sea / lakes / rivers etc.
6	Green Procurement policy	XX	Whether the company's procurement policy has given adequate emphasis for green procurement, eco labelling, local purchase, environment compatible / recyclable packaging, take back / buy back ,4R - Reduce, Reuse, Recycle and Responsible disposal. If yes, % compared to total procurement. Whether the company has initiated steps for paper usage reduction and promotion of digitalisation. If yes, % of saving in paper consumption
	Evaluation Score (Average)	XX	

APPENDIX B

Evaluation Score - Social (Year)			
Country			
No.	**Item Head**	**Percentage**	**Guidelines**
1	People	XX	Does the company has Diversity, Equality & Inclusion (DEI) Policy commiserating with the size of the entity. Does DEI policy includes work life balance, team work, respectful communication, community engagement (including social media, local public) , various diversities viz racial, religious, sexual , gender, age , physical disability etc Does the DEI policy includes fair pay and living wages, equal employment opportunities, employee benefit, adherence to labour laws, opportunity for learning and development, leadership development, succession planning, employee engagement and feedback. Does any deviations to the policy has been reported in the year. If yes, whether corrective action has been taken. CSR policy, implementation and outcomes, beneficiaries
2	Health & Safety	XX	Does the company have a health & safety policy in line with the freight forwarding industry. Does the policy has been updated with respect to recent developments (eg. Hand sanitation etc during COVID period) Does any deviations to the policy has been reported in the year. If yes, whether corrective action has been taken. Whether the company has a disaster management team (DMT). Do they conduct mock drills, if yes how many in last one year.
3	Human Rights Policy	XX	Does the company have a Human Rights policy. Does any deviations to the policy has been reported in the year. If yes, whether corrective action has been taken.
4	Customer experience / satisfaction	XX	Does the company have invested in online tools for receiving supplier feedback. Whether there is a periodic review on customer feedback Whether necessary corrective actions / improvements have been initiated based on customer feedback.
5	Rural transformation	XX	Whether the company have a policy for rural employment, viz office in rural areas / giving priority for employees from rural area, if yes, what %
6	Grievance redressal of all stake holders (Shareholders, customers, employees etc)	XX	Whether the company have a system of confidential reporting, if yes how many complains received and actioned. Whether the company has a whistle blower policy, if yes how much information's received and actioned. How is the whistle blower protected.
	Evaluation Score (Average)	XX	

APPENDIX C

Evaluation Score - Governance (Year)			
Country:			
No.	Item Head	Percentage	Guidelines
1	Code of Conduct	XX	Does the company have a written Code of Conduct. How efficient is the CoC implementation viz violation (if any) and corrective actions dealt with. Does the company have taken initiatives for educating employees on CoC Does CoC have periodic revision with respect to statutory requirement and technological upgradation
2	Good Practices	XX	Does the company have a written anti bribery policy (including gifts, donations & political lobbying, corruption, scandal etc). How efficient is the policy implementation viz deviation (if any) and disciplinary action dealt with. How many cases reported. Does the company have taken initiatives for educating employees on Anti Bribery policy Does policy have periodic revision with respect technological upgradation viz online payments, freebees etc
3	Cyber security	XX	Does the company have an IT policy covering cyber / information security. Does the company has an SOP for regular data backup and storage Whether there is a periodic review of IT policy and updating based on technological advancement Any violation of policy reported. Whether necessary corrective actions / improvements have been initiated based on the review
4	Privacy Policy	XX	Does the company have Privacy policy. Does the company has the practice of getting confidentiality agreement signed by all stake holders (employee, customer, vendor etc). Whether there is a periodic review on privacy policy violation (if any) and necessary corrective actions / improvements has been initiated based on the review"
5	BCP - Business Continuity Plan	XX	Whether the company has a Business Continuity plan (BCP) to face contingency, so that the going concern principle of the entity is not affected. Does the entity has a disaster management plan (DMP) to face any Act of God. Does there is a periodic review of BCP and DMP. Whether necessary upgradation / changes have been initiated based on the previous experience or technological changes.
6	Compliance	XX	Whether the company has a written corporate governance principle which includes transparency, accountability, security etc towards all stake holders. Does it includes constitution of committees for audit, shareholders engagement, compensation, CSR, environment awareness etc. Tax evasion should be strictly dealt with whereas tax planning is permitted. The committees should ensure that all the statutory compliances has been strictly followed. Frequency of the committee meeting and attendance of the members should be reviewed. Deviations / violations must be listed, and action taken should be checked
	Evaluation Score (Average)	XX	

BIBLIOGRAPHY

BOOKS & JOURNALS

- Billio, M., Costola, M., Hristova, I., Latino, C., & Pelizzon, L. (2021). Inside the ESG ratings:(Dis) agreement and performance. *Corporate Social Responsibility and Environmental Management, 28*(5), 1426-1445.
- Christensen, D. M., Serafeim, G., & Sikochi, A. (2022). Why is corporate virtue in the eye of the beholder? The case of ESG ratings. *The Accounting Review, 97*(1), 147-175.
- Gibson Brandon, R., Krueger, P., & Schmidt, P. S. (2021). ESG rating disagreement and stock returns. *Financial analysts journal, 77*(4), 104-127.
- Intergovernmental panel on climate change (IPCC), (2023) , *Synthesis Report,* https://www.ipcc.ch
- Lean, H. H., Huang, W., & Hong, J. (2014). Logistics and economic development: Experience from China. *Transport policy, 32*, 96-104.
- Larry Swedroe, (2021) , *Do wide divergences in ESG ratings doom investors,* www.advisorperspectives.com
- United Nation, (2004), *Who Cares Wins,* www. https://www.unepfi.org
- World Economic forum, (2022), *Defining the 'G' in ESG Governance Factors at the Heart of Sustainable Business,* https://www3.weforum.org
- Mackintosh, J.: 2018, Is Tesla or Exxon more sustainable? It depends whom you ask, Wall Street Journal. URL: https://on.wsj.com/2MQCC4m

WEBSITES & INTERNET SOURCES

- https://www.epi.yale.edu
- https://www.ghgprotocol.org
- https://www.hdr.undp.org
- https://iriscarbon.com/a-beginners-guide-to-esg-rating-agencies-and-methodologies

- https://www.socialprogress.org
- https://www.solability.com
- https://www.sdgs.un.org/goals#icons
- https://www.statista.com/statistics
- https://www.un.org
- https://www.unfccc.int
- https://www.worldbank.org

www.ingramcontent.com/pod-product-compliance
Lightning Source LLC
LaVergne TN
LVHW022053200926
848481LV00003B/899
9798904513665